W9-BDN-174

THE SIXTH AMENDMENT

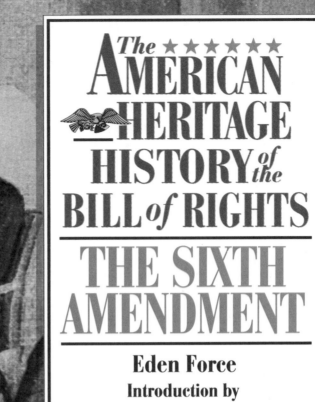

The ★★★★★★★
AMERICAN
HERITAGE
HISTORY of the
BILL of RIGHTS

THE SIXTH
AMENDMENT

Eden Force

Introduction by
WARREN E. BURGER
Chief Justice of the United States
1969–1986

Silver Burdett Press

To Robert, with thanks for his encouragement.

Cover: In scenes similar to this across the United States, citizens exercise many of their Sixth Amendment rights such as the rights to a speedy and public trial by impartial jury.

CONSULTANTS:

Jessie B. Gladden
Divisional Specialist
Office of Social Studies
Baltimore City Schools
Baltimore, Maryland

Michael H. Reggio
Law-Related Education
 Coordinator
Oklahoma Bar Association
Oklahoma City, Oklahoma

Herbert Sloan
Assistant Professor of History
Barnard College
New York, New York

Text and Cover Design: Circa 86, Inc.

Copyright © 1991 by Gallin House Press, Inc.
Introduction copyright © 1991 by Silver Burdett Press, Inc.

All rights reserved, including the right of reproduction in whole or in part in any form.
Published by Silver Burdett Press, Inc., a division of Simon & Schuster, Inc., Englewood Cliffs, N.J. 07632.

Library of Congress Cataloging-in-Publication Data

Force, Eden,
    The Sixth Amendment/by Eden Force: with an introduction by Warren E. Burger.
    p. cm.—(The American Heritage history of the Bill of Rights)
    Includes bibliographical references and indexes.
    Summary: Studies the historical origins of provisions of the Sixth Amendment, which guarantees certain rights of trial to persons accused of crimes.
    1. United States—Constitutional law—Amendments—6th—History—
Juvenile literature. 2. Speedy trial—United States—History—
Juvenile literature. 3. Fair trial—United States—History—
Juvenile literature. 4. Jury—United States—History—Juvenile
literature. 5. Right to counsel—United States—History—Juvenile
literature. {1. United States—Constitutional law—
Amendments—6th—History. 2. Civil rights—History.} I. Title.
II. Series.
KF4558 6th. F67 1991
345. 73'056—dc20
{347.30556}

90-19296
CIP
AC

Manufactured in the United States of America.
ISBN 0-382-24184-3 {lib. bdg.}
10 9 8 7 6 5 4 3 2 1

ISBN 0-382-24197-5 {pbk.}
10 9 8 7 6 5 4 3 2 1

$\mathscr{C}$ONTENTS

$\mathcal{I}$ NTRODUCTION

WARREN E. BURGER
Chief Justice of the United States, 1969–1986

The Sixth Amendment guarantees important rights to persons accused of a crime: the right to trial by jury, the right to compel the appearance of witnesses for the defense, and the right to a lawyer. These rights are specific implements of a more general concept of liberty that is fundamental to the American people.

Concepts of liberty—the values liberty protects—inspired the Framers of our Constitution and the Bill of Rights to some of their most impassioned eloquence. "Liberty, the greatest of earthly possessions—give us that precious jewel, and you may take everything else," declaimed Patrick Henry. Those toilers in the "vineyard of liberty" sensed the historic nature of their mission, and their foresight accounts for the survival of the Bill of Rights.

Today, courts and citizens must work together to preserve the principles of the Sixth Amendment. Trial by jury is perhaps the most important barrier between the citizen and government. Jury service is an obligation of every citizen and is an experience that makes most jurors understand the fairness and seriousness of our judicial system.

The long-term success of the system of ordered liberty set up by our Constitution was by no means foreordained. The bicentennial of the Bill of Rights provides an opportunity to reflect on the significance of the freedoms we enjoy and to commit ourselves to exercise the civic responsibilities required to sustain our constitutional system. The Constitution, including its first ten amendments, the Bill of Rights, has survived two centuries because of its unprecedented philosophical premise: that it derives its power from the people. It is not a grant from the government to the people. In 1787 the masters—the people—were saying to their government—their servant—that certain rights are inherent, natural rights and that they belong to the people, who had those rights before any governments existed. The function of government, they said, was to protect these rights.

The Bill of Rights also owes its continued vitality to the fact that it was drafted by experienced, practical politicians. It was a product of the Framers' essential mistrust of the frailties of human nature. This led them to develop the idea of the separation of powers and to make the Bill of Rights part of the permanent Constitution.

Moreover, the document was designed to be flexible, and the role of providing that flexibility through interpretation has fallen to the judiciary. Indeed, the first commander in chief, George Washington, gave the Supreme Court its moral marching orders two centuries ago when he said, "the administration of justice is the firmest pillar of government." The principle of judicial review as a check on government has perhaps nowhere been more significant than in the protection of individual liberties. It has been my privilege, along with my colleagues on the Court, to ensure the continued vitality of our Bill of Rights. As John Marshall asked, long before he became chief justice, "To what quarter will you look for a protection from an infringement on the Constitution, if you will not give the power to the judiciary?"

But the preservation of the Bill of Rights is not the sole responsibility of the judiciary. Rather, judges, legislatures, and presidents are partners with every American; liberty is the responsibility of every public officer and every citizen. In this spirit all Americans should become acquainted with the principles and history of this most remarkable document. Its bicentennial should not be simply a celebration but the beginning of an ongoing process. Americans must—by their conduct—guarantee that it continues to protect the sacred rights of our uniquely multicultural population. We must not fail to exercise our rights to vote, to participate in government and community activities, and to implement the principles of liberty, tolerance, opportunity, and justice for all.

T H E A M E R I C A N H E R I T A G E
HISTORY OF THE BILL OF RIGHTS

THE FIRST AMENDMENT
by Philip A. Klinkner

THE SECOND AMENDMENT
by Joan C. Hawxhurst

THE THIRD AMENDMENT
by Burnham Holmes

THE FOURTH AMENDMENT
by Paula A. Franklin

THE FIFTH AMENDMENT
by Burnham Holmes

THE SIXTH AMENDMENT
by Eden Force

THE SEVENTH AMENDMENT
by Lila E. Summer

THE EIGHTH AMENDMENT
by Vincent Buranelli

THE NINTH AMENDMENT
by Philip A. Klinkner

THE TENTH AMENDMENT
by Judith Adams

The Bill of Rights

AMENDMENT 1*
Article Congress shall make no law respecting an establishment of religion, or prohibiting the free exercise thereof; or abridging the freedom of speech, or of the press; or the right of the people peaceably to assemble, and to petition the Government for a redress of grievances.

AMENDMENT 2
Article A well regulated Militia, being necessary to the security of a free State, the right of the people to keep and bear Arms, shall not be infringed.

AMENDMENT 3
Article No Soldier shall, in time of peace be quartered in any house, without the consent of the Owner, nor in time of war, but in a manner to be prescribed by law.

AMENDMENT 4
Article The right of the people to be secure in their persons, houses, papers, and effects, against unreasonable searches and seizures, shall not be violated, and no Warrants shall issue, but upon probable cause, supported by Oath or affirmation, and particularly describing the place to be searched, and the persons or things to be seized.

AMENDMENT 5
Article No person shall be held to answer for a capital, or otherwise infamous crime, unless on a presentment or indictment of a Grand Jury, except in cases arising in the land or naval forces, or in the Militia, when in actual service in time of War or public danger; nor shall any person be subject for the same offence to be twice put in jeopardy of life or limb; nor shall be compelled in any criminal case to be a witness against himself, nor be deprived of life, liberty, or property, without due process of law; nor shall private property be taken for public use without just compensation.

AMENDMENT 6
Article In all criminal prosecutions, the accused shall enjoy the right to a speedy and public trial, by an impartial jury of the State and district wherein the crime shall have been committed, which district shall have been previously ascertained by law, and to be informed of the nature and cause of the accusation; to be confronted with the witnesses against him; to have compulsory process for obtaining Witnesses in his favor, and to have the assistance of counsel for his defence.

AMENDMENT 7
Article In Suits at common law, where the value in controversy shall exceed twenty dollars, the right of trial by jury shall be preserved, and no fact tried by a jury, shall be otherwise reexamined in any Court of the United States, than according to the rules of the common law.

AMENDMENT 8
Article Excessive bail shall not be required, nor excessive fines imposed, nor cruel and unusual punishments inflicted.

AMENDMENT 9
Article The enumeration in the Constitution, of certain rights, shall not be construed to deny or disparage others retained by the people.

AMENDMENT 10
Article The powers not delegated to the United States by the Constitution, nor prohibited by it to the States, are reserved to the States respectively, or to the people.

*Note that each of the first ten amendments to the original Constitution is called an "Article." None of these amendments had actual numbers at the time of their ratification.

THE HISTORY OF THE
BILL OF RIGHTS

1770s–1790s

1774 Quartering Act
1775 Revolutionary War begins
1776 Declaration of Independence is signed.
1783 Revolutionary War ends.
1787 Constitutional Convention writes the U.S. Constitution.
1788 U.S. Constitution is ratified by most states.
1789 Congress proposes the Bill of Rights
1791 The Bill of Rights is ratified by the states.
1792 Militia Act

1800s–1820s

1803 *Marbury* v. *Madison*. Supreme Court declares that it has the power of judicial review and exercises it. This is the first case in which the Court holds a law of Congress unconstitutional.
1807 Trial of Aaron Burr. Ruling that juries may have knowledge of a case so long as they have not yet formed an opinion.
1813 Kentucky becomes the first state to outlaw concealed weapons.
1824 *Gibbons* v. *Ogden*. Supreme Court defines Congress's power to regulate commerce, including trade between states and within states if that commerce affects other states.

1830s–1870s

1833 *Barron* v. *Baltimore*. Supreme Court rules that Bill of Rights applies only to actions of the federal government, not to the states and local governments.

1851 *Cooley* v. *Board of Wardens of the Port of Philadelphia*. Supreme Court rules that states can apply their own rules to some foreign and interstate commerce if their rules are of a local nature—unless or until Congress makes rules for particular situations.

1857 *Dred Scott* v. *Sandford*. Supreme Court denies that African Americans are citizens even if they happen to live in a "free state."

1862 Militia Act

1865 Thirteenth Amendment is ratified. Slavery is not allowed in the United States.

1868 Fourteenth Amendment is ratified. All people born or naturalized in the United States are citizens. Their privileges and immunities are protected, as are their life, liberty, and property according to due process. They have equal protection of the laws.

1873 *Slaughterhouse* cases. Supreme Court rules that the Fourteenth Amendment does not limit state power to make laws dealing with economic matters. Court mentions the unenumerated right to political participation.

1876 *United States* v. *Cruikshank*. Supreme Court rules that the right to bear arms for a lawful purpose is not an absolute right granted by the Constitution. States can limit this right and make their own gun-control laws.

1880s–1920s

1884 *Hurtado* v. *California*. Supreme Court rules that the right to a grand jury indictment doesn't apply to the states.

1896 *Plessy* v. *Ferguson*. Supreme Court upholds a state law based on "separate but equal" facilities for different races.

1903 Militia Act creates National Guard.

1905 *Lochner* v. *New York*. Supreme Court strikes down a state law regulating maximum work hours.

1914 *Weeks* v. *United States*. Supreme Court establishes that illegally obtained evidence, obtained by unreasonable search and seizure, cannot be used in federal trials.

1918 *Hammer* v. *Dagenhart*. Supreme Court declares unconstitutional a federal law prohibiting the shipment between states of goods made by young children.

1923 *Meyer* v. *Nebraska*. Supreme Court rules that a law banning teaching of foreign languages or teaching in languages other than English is unconstitutional. Court says that certain areas of people's private lives are protected from government interference.

1925 *Carroll* v. *United States*. Supreme Court allows searches of automobiles without a search warrant under some circumstances.

1925 *Gitlow* v. *New York*. Supreme Court rules that freedom of speech and freedom of the press are protected from state actions by the Fourteenth Amendment.

1930s

1931 *Near* v. *Minnesota*. Supreme Court rules that liberty of the press and of speech are safeguarded from state action.

1931 *Stromberg* v. *California*. Supreme Court extends concept of freedom of speech to symbolic actions such as displaying a flag.

1932 *Powell* v. *Alabama* (*First Scottsboro* case). Supreme Court rules that poor defendants have a right to an appointed lawyer when tried for crimes that may result in the death penalty.

1934 National Firearms Act becomes the first federal law to restrict the keeping and bearing of arms.

1935 *Norris* v. *Alabama* (*Second Scottsboro* case). Supreme Court reverses the conviction of an African American because of the long continued excluding of African Americans from jury service in the trial area.

1937 *Palko* v. *Connecticut*. Supreme Court refuses to require states to protect people under the double jeopardy clause of the Bill of Rights. But the case leads to future application of individual rights in the Bill of Rights to the states on a case-by-case basis.

1937 *DeJonge* v. *Oregon*. Supreme Court rules that freedom of assembly and petition are protected against state laws.

1939 *United States* v. *Miller*. Supreme Court rules that National Firearms Act of 1934 does not violate Second Amendment.

1940s–1950s

1940 *Cantwell* v. *Connecticut*. Supreme Court rules that free exercise of religion is protected against state laws.

1943 *Barnette* v. *West Virginia State Board of Education*. Supreme Court rules that flag salute laws are unconstitutional.

1946 *Theil* v. *Pacific Railroad*. Juries must be a cross section of the community, excluding no group based on religion, race, sex, or economic status.

1947 *Everson* v. *Board of Education*. Supreme Court rules that government attempts to impose religious practices, the establishment of religion, is forbidden to the states.

1948 *In re Oliver*. Supreme Court rules that defendants have a right to public trial in nonfederal trials.

1949 *Wolf* v. *California*. Supreme Court rules that freedom from unreasonable searches and seizures also applies to states.

1954 *Brown* v. *Board of Education of Topeka*. Supreme Court holds that segregation on the basis of race (in public education) denies equal protection of the laws.

1958 *NAACP* v. *Alabama*. Supreme Court rules that the privacy of membership lists in an organization is part of the right to freedom of assembly and association.

1960s

1961 *Mapp* v. *Ohio.* Supreme Court rules that illegally obtained evidence must not be allowed in state criminal trials.

1962 *Engel* v. *Vitale.* Supreme Court strikes down state-sponsored school prayer, saying it is no business of government to compose official prayers as part of a religious program carried on by the government.

1963 *Gideon* v. *Wainwright.* Supreme Court rules that the right of people accused of serious crimes to be represented by an appointed counsel applies to state criminal trials.

1964 Civil Rights Act is passed.

1964 *Malloy* v. *Hogan.* Supreme Court rules that the right to protection against forced self-incrimination applies to state trials.

1965 *Griswold* v. *Connecticut.* Supreme Court rules that there is a right to privacy in marriage and declares unconstitutional a state law banning the use of or the giving of information about birth control.

1965 *Pointer* v. *Texas.* Supreme Court rules that the right to confront witnesses against an accused person applies to state trials.

1966 *Parker* v. *Gladden.* Supreme Court ruling is interpreted to mean that the right to an impartial jury is applied to the states.

1966 *Miranda* v. *Arizona.* Supreme Court extends the protection against forced self-incrimination. Police have to inform people in custody of their rights before questioning them.

1967 *Katz* v. *United States.* Supreme Court rules that people's right to be free of unreasonable searches includes protection against electronic surveillance.

1967 *Washington* v. *Texas.* Supreme Court rules that accused people have the right to have witnesses in their favor brought into court.

1967 *In re Gault.* Supreme Court rules that juvenile proceedings that might lead to the young person's being sent to a state institution must follow due process and fair treatment. These include the rights against forced self-incrimination, to counsel, to confront witnesses.

1967 *Klopfer* v. *North Carolina.* Supreme Court rules that the right to a speedy trial applies to state trials.

1968 *Duncan* v. *Louisiana.* Supreme Court rules that the right to a jury trial in criminal cases applies to state trials.

1969 *Benton* v. *Maryland.* Supreme Court rules that the protection against double jeopardy applies to the states.

1969 *Brandenburg* v. *Ohio.* Supreme Court rules that speech calling for the use of force or crime can only be prohibited if it is directed to bringing about immediate lawless action and is likely to bring about such action.

1970s–1990s

1970 *Williams* v. *Florida.* Juries in cases that do not lead to the possibility of the death penalty may consist of six jurors rather than twelve.

1971 *Pentagon Papers* case. Freedom of the press is protected by forbidding prior restraint.

1971 *Duke Power Co.* v. *Carolina Environmental Study Group, Inc.* Supreme Court upholds state law limiting liability of federally licensed power companies in the event of a nuclear accident.

1972 *Furman* v. *Georgia.* Supreme Court rules that the death penalty (as it was then decided upon) is cruel and unusual punishment and therefore unconstitutional.

1972 *Argersinger* v. *Hamlin.* Supreme Court rules that right to counsel applies to all criminal cases that might involve a jail term.

1973 *Roe* v. *Wade.* Supreme Court declares that the right to privacy protects a woman's right to end pregnancy by abortion under specified circumstances.

1976 *Gregg* v. *Georgia.* Supreme Court rules that the death penalty is to be allowed if it is decided upon in a consistent and reasonable way, if the sentencing follows strict guidelines, and if the penalty is not required for certain crimes.

1976 *National League of Cities* v. *Usery.* Supreme Court holds that the Tenth Amendment prevents Congress from making federal minimum wage and overtime rules apply to state and city workers.

1981 *Quilici* v. *Village of Morton Grove.* U.S. district court upholds a local ban on sale and possession of handguns.

1985 *Garcia* v. *San Antonio Metropolitan Transit Authority.* Supreme Court rules that Congress can make laws dealing with wages and hour rules applied to city-owned transportation systems.

1989 *Webster* v. *Reproductive Health Services.* Supreme Court holds that a state may prohibit all use of public facilities and publicly employed staff in abortions.

1989 *Johnson* v. *Texas.* Supreme Court rules that flag burning is protected and is a form of "symbolic speech."

1990 *Cruzan* v. *Missouri Department of Health.* Supreme Court recognizes for the first time a very sick person's right to die without being forced to undergo unwanted medical treatment and a person's right to a living will.

1990 *Noriega–CNN* case. Supreme Court upholds lower federal court's decision to allow temporary prior restraint thus limiting the First Amendment right of freedom of the press.

The Birth of the Bill of Rights

"We hold these truths to be self-evident, that all men are created equal, that they are endowed by their Creator with certain unalienable Rights, that among these are Life, Liberty, and the pursuit of Happiness."

THE DECLARATION OF INDEPENDENCE (1776)

A brave Chinese student standing in front of a line of tanks, Eastern Europeans marching against the secret police, happy crowds dancing on top of the Berlin Wall—these were recent scenes of people trying to gain their freedom or celebrating it. The scenes and the events that sparked them will live on in history. They also show the lasting gift that is our Bill of Rights. The freedoms guaranteed by the Bill of Rights have guided and inspired millions of people all over the world in their struggle for freedom.

The Colonies Gain Their Freedom

Like many countries today, the United States fought to gain freedom and democracy for itself. The American colonies had a revolution from 1775 to 1783 to free themselves from British rule.

The colonists fought to free themselves because they believed that the British had violated, or gone against, their rights. The colonists held what some considered the extreme idea that all

James Madison is known as both the "Father of the Constitution" and the "Father of the Bill of Rights." In 1789 he proposed to Congress the amendments that became the Bill of Rights. Madison served two terms as president of the United States from 1809 to 1817.

The Raising of the Liberty Pole by John McRae. In 1776, American colonists hoisted liberty poles as symbols of liberty and freedom from British rule. At the top they usually placed a liberty cap. Such caps resembled the caps given to slaves in ancient Rome when they were freed.

persons are born with certain rights. They believed that these rights could not be taken away, even by the government. The importance our nation gave to individual rights can be seen in the Declaration of Independence. The Declaration, written by Thomas Jefferson in 1776, states:

> We hold these truths to be self-evident, that all men are created equal, that they are endowed by their Creator with certain unaliena-ble Rights, that among these are Life, Liberty, and the pursuit of Happiness.

The United States won its independence from Britain in 1783. But with freedom came the difficult job of forming a government. The Americans wanted a government that was strong enough to keep peace and prosperity, but not so strong that it might take away the rights for which the Revolution had been fought. The Articles of Confederation was the country's first written plan of government.

The Articles of Confederation, becoming law in 1781, created a weak national government. The defects in the Articles soon became clear to many Americans. Because the United States did not have a strong national government, its economy suffered. Under the Articles, Congress did not have the power to tax. It had to ask the states for money or borrow it. There was no separate president or court system. Nine of the states had to agree before Congress's bills became law. In 1786 economic problems caused farmers in Massachusetts to revolt. The national government was almost powerless to stop the revolt. It was also unable to build an army or navy strong enough to protect the United States's borders and its ships on the high seas.

The Constitution Is Drawn Up

The nation's problems had to be solved. So, in February 1787, the Continental Congress asked the states to send delegates to a convention to discuss ways of improving the Articles. That May, fifty-five delegates, from every state except Rhode Island, met in Philadelphia. The group included some of the country's most famous leaders: George Washington, hero of the Revolution; Benjamin Franklin, publisher, inventor, and diplomat; and James Madison, a leading critic of the Articles. Madison would soon become the guiding force behind the Constitutional Convention.

After a long, hot summer of debate the delegates finally drew up the document that became the U.S. Constitution. It set up a strong central government. But it also divided power between three branches of the federal government. These three branches were the executive branch (the presidency), the legislative branch (Congress), and the judicial branch (the courts). Each was given one part of the government's power. This division was to make sure that no single branch became so powerful that it could violate the people's rights.

The legislative branch (made up of the House of Representatives and the Senate) would have the power to pass laws, raise taxes and spend money, regulate the national economy, and declare war. The executive branch was given the power to carry out the laws, run foreign affairs, and command the military.

The Signing of the Constitution painted by Thomas Rossiter. The Constitutional Convention met in Philadelphia from May into September 1787. The proposed Constitution contained protection for some individual rights such as protection against *ex post facto* laws and bills of attainder. When the Constitution was ratified by the required number of states in 1788, however, it did not have a bill of rights.

The role of the judicial branch in this plan was less clear. The Constitution said that the judicial branch would have "judicial power." However, it was unclear exactly what this power was. Over the years "judicial power" has come to mean "judicial review." The power of judicial review allows the federal courts to reject laws passed by Congress or the state legislatures that they believe violate the Constitution.

Judicial review helps protect our rights. It allows federal courts to reject laws that violate the Constitution's guarantees of individual rights. Because of this power, James Madison believed that the courts would be an "impenetrable bulwark," an unbreakable wall, against any attempt by government to take away these rights.

The Constitution did more than divide the power of the federal government among the three branches. It also divided power between the states and the federal government. This division of power is known as *federalism*. Federalism means that the federal

government has control over certain areas. These include regulating the national economy and running foreign and military affairs. The states have control over most other areas. For example, they regulate their economies and make most other laws. Once again, the Framers (writers) of the Constitution hoped that the division of powers would keep both the states and the federal government from becoming too strong and possibly violating individual rights.

The new Constitution did *not,* however, contain a bill of rights. Such a bill would list the people's rights and would forbid the government from interfering with them. The only discussion of the topic came late in the convention. At that time, George Mason of Virginia called for a bill of rights. A Connecticut delegate, Roger Sherman, disagreed. He claimed that a bill of rights was not needed. In his view, the Constitution did not take away any of the rights in the bills of rights in the state constitutions. These had been put in place during the Revolution. The other delegates agreed with Roger Sherman. Mason's proposal was voted down by all.

Yet the Constitution was not without guarantees of individual rights. One of these rights was the protection of *habeas corpus.* This is a legal term that refers to the right of someone who has been arrested to be brought into court and formally charged with a crime. Another right forbade *ex post facto* laws. These are laws that outlaw actions that took place before the passage of the laws. Other parts of the Constitution forbade bills of attainder (laws pronouncing a person guilty of a crime without trial), required jury trials, restricted convictions for treason, and guaranteed a republican form of government. That is a government in which political power rests with citizens who vote for elected officials and representatives responsible to the voters. The Constitution also forbade making public officials pass any "religious test." This meant that religious requirements could not be forced on public officials.

The Debate Over the New Constitution

Once it was written, the Constitution had to be ratified, or approved, by nine of the states before it could go into effect. The new

Constitution created much controversy. Heated battles raged in many states over whether or not to approve the document. One of the main arguments used by those who opposed the Constitution (the Anti-Federalists) was that the Constitution made the federal government too strong. They feared that it might violate the rights of the people just as the British government had. Although he had helped write the Constitution, Anti-Federalist George Mason opposed it for this reason. He claimed that he would sooner chop off his right hand than put it to the Constitution as it then stood.

To correct what they viewed as flaws in the Constitution, the Anti-Federalists insisted that it have a bill of rights. The fiery orator of the Revolution, Patrick Henry, another Anti-Federalist, exclaimed, "Liberty, the greatest of all earthly blessings—give us that precious jewel, and you may take every thing else!"

Although he was not an Anti-Federalist, Thomas Jefferson also believed that a bill of rights was needed. He wrote a letter to James Madison, a wavering Federalist, in which he said: "A bill of rights is what the people are entitled to against every government on earth."

Supporters of the Constitution (the Federalists) argued that it did not need a bill of rights. One reason they stated, similar to that given at the Philadelphia convention, was that most state constitutions had a bill of rights. Nothing in the Constitution would limit or abolish these rights. In 1788 James Madison wrote that he thought a bill of rights would provide only weak "parchment barriers" against attempts by government to take away individual rights. He believed that history had shown that a bill of rights was ineffective on "those occasions when its control [was] needed most."

The views of the Anti-Federalists seem to have had more support than did those of the Federalists. The Federalists came to realize that without a bill of rights, the states might not approve the new Constitution. To ensure ratification, the Federalists therefore agreed to support adding a bill of rights to the Constitution.

With this compromise, eleven of the thirteen states ratified the Constitution by July 1788. The new government of the United States was born. The two remaining states, North Carolina and

Rhode Island, in time accepted the new Constitution. North Carolina approved it in November 1789 and Rhode Island in May 1790.

James Madison Calls for a Bill of Rights

On April 30, 1789, George Washington took the oath of office as president. The new government was launched. One of its first jobs was to amend, or change, the Constitution to include a bill of rights. This is what many of the states had called for during the ratification process. Leading this effort in the new Congress was James Madison. He was a strong supporter of individual rights. As a member of the Virginia legislature, he had helped frame the Virginia Declaration of Rights. He had also fought for religious liberty.

Madison, however, had at first opposed including a bill of rights. But his views had changed. He feared that the Constitution would not be ratified by enough states to become law unless the Federalists offered to include a bill of rights. Madison also knew that many people were afraid of the new government. He feared they might oppose its actions or attempt to undo it. He said a bill of rights "will kill the opposition everywhere, and by putting an end to disaffection to [discontent with] the Government itself, enable the administration to venture on measures not otherwise safe."

On June 8, 1789, the thirty-eight-year-old Madison rose to speak in the House of Representatives. He called for several changes to the Constitution that contained the basis of our present Bill of Rights. Despite his powerful words, Madison's speech did not excite his listeners. Most Federalists in Congress opposed a bill of rights. Others believed that the new Constitution should be given more time to operate before Congress considered making any changes. Many Anti-Federalists wanted a new constitutional convention. There, they hoped to greatly limit the powers of the federal government. These Anti-Federalists thought that adding a bill of rights to the Constitution would prevent their movement for a new convention.

Finally, in August, Madison persuaded the House to consider

his amendments. The House accepted most of them. However, instead of being placed in the relevant sections of the Constitution, as Madison had called for, the House voted to add them as separate amendments. This change—listing the amendments together—made the Bill of Rights the distinct document that it is today.

After approval by the House, the amendments went to the Senate. The Senate dropped what Madison considered the most important part of his plan. This was the protection of freedom of the press, freedom of religious belief, and the right to trial by jury from violation by the states. Protection of these rights from violation by state governments would have to wait until after the Fourteenth Amendment was adopted in 1868.

The House and the Senate at last agreed on ten amendments to protect individual rights. What rights were protected? Here is a partial list:

The First Amendment protects freedom of religion, of speech, of the press, of peaceful assembly, and of petition.

The Second Amendment gives to the states the right to keep a militia (a volunteer, reserve military force) and to the people the right to keep and bear arms.

The Third Amendment prevents the government from keeping troops in private homes during wartime.

The Fourth Amendment protects individuals from unreasonable searches and seizures by the government.

The Fifth Amendment states that the government must get an indictment (an official ruling that a crime has been committed) before someone can be tried for a serious crime. This amendment bans "double jeopardy." This means trying a person twice for the same criminal offense. It also protects people from having to testify against themselves in court.

The Fifth Amendment also says that the government cannot take away a person's "life, liberty, or property, without due process of law." This means that the government must follow fair and just procedures if it takes away a person's "life, liberty, or property." Finally, the Fifth Amendment says that if the government takes property from an individual for public use, it must pay that person an adequate sum of money for the property.

The Sixth Amendment requires that all criminal trials be speedy and public, and decided by a fair jury. The amendment also allows people on trial to know what offense they have been charged with. It also allows them to be present when others testify against them, to call witnesses to their defense, and to have the help of a lawyer.

The Seventh Amendment provides for a jury trial in all cases involving amounts over $20.

The Eighth Amendment forbids unreasonably high bail (money paid to free someone from jail before his or her trial), unreasonably large fines, and cruel and unusual punishments.

The Ninth Amendment says that the rights of the people are not limited only to those listed in the Bill of Rights.

Finally, the Tenth Amendment helps to establish federalism by giving to the states and the people any powers not given to the federal government by the Constitution.

After being approved by the House and the Senate, the amendments were sent to the states for adoption in October 1789. By December 1791, three-fourths of the states had approved the ten amendments we now know as the Bill of Rights. The Bill of Rights had become part of the U.S. Constitution.

How Our Court System Works

Many of the events in this book concern court cases involving the Bill of Rights. To help understand how the U.S. court system works, here is a brief description.

The U.S. federal court system has three levels. At the lowest level are the federal district courts. There are ninety-four district courts, each covering a different area of the United States and its territories. Most cases having to do with the Constitution begin in the district courts.

People who lose their cases in the district courts may then appeal to the next level in the court system, the federal courts of appeals. To appeal means to take your case to a higher court in an attempt to change the lower court's decision. Here, those who are making the appeal try to obtain a different judgment. There are thirteen federal courts of appeals in the United States.

People who lose in the federal courts of appeals may then take their case to the U.S. Supreme Court. It is the highest court in the land. The Supreme Court has the final say in a case. You cannot appeal a Supreme Court decision.

The size of the Supreme Court is set by Congress and has changed over the years. Since 1869 the Supreme Court has been made up of nine justices. One is the chief justice of the United States, and eight are associate justices. The justices are named by the president and confirmed by the Senate.

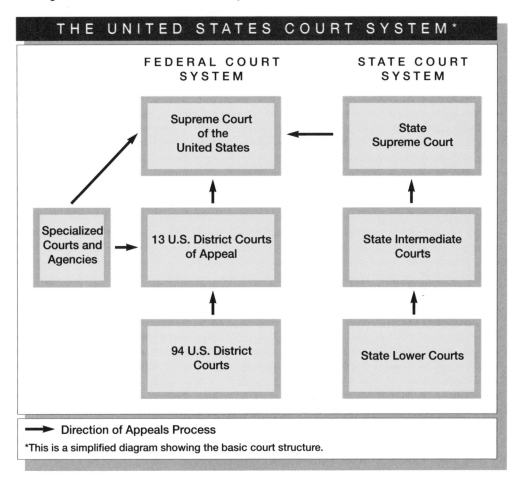

THE UNITED STATES COURT SYSTEM*

FEDERAL COURT SYSTEM

STATE COURT SYSTEM

Supreme Court of the United States ← State Supreme Court

Specialized Courts and Agencies → 13 U.S. District Courts of Appeal

State Intermediate Courts

94 U.S. District Courts

State Lower Courts

→ Direction of Appeals Process

*This is a simplified diagram showing the basic court structure.

In the Supreme Court, a simple majority of votes is needed to decide a case. If there is a tie, the lower court's decision remains in effect. When the chief justice votes on the majority side, he or she can assign the writing of the opinion to any of the majority justices, including himself or herself. The opinion states the Court's decision and the reasons for it. Who writes the opinion when the chief justice hasn't voted on the majority side? In that case, the longest-serving associate justice who voted for the majority decision can assign the writing to any of the majority justices, including himself or herself.

What if a justice has voted for the majority decision but doesn't agree with the reasons given in the majority opinion? He or she may write what is called a concurring opinion. That is one which agrees with the Court's decision but for different reasons.

Those justices who disagree with the Court's decision may write what is called a dissenting opinion. They have the opportunity to explain why they think the majority Supreme Court decision is wrong.

In addition to the federal court system, each state has its own system of courts. These systems vary from state to state. However, they are usually made up of two or three levels of lower courts and then the state's highest court, usually called the state supreme court. Those who lose their cases in the state supreme court may appeal those decisions to the federal court system, usually to the Supreme Court.

Not all cases that are appealed to the Supreme Court are heard by it. In fact, very few of them are. For the Supreme Court to decide to hear a case, four of the nine justices must vote to hear it. If fewer than four justices vote to hear the case, then the judgment of the lower court remains in effect.

The Sixth Amendment

This book is about the Sixth Amendment. It is one of the three Bill of Rights amendments that guarantees the rights which people have if they are accused of a crime. (The Fourth and Fifth Amendments also guarantee some of the rights of people who are accused of crimes.) This book tells how the Sixth Amendment has been interpreted over the years, what controversies have swirled around it, and how it has affected the lives of Americans.

PHILIP A. KLINKNER

The Background of the Sixth Amendment

"The trial of all crimes, except in cases of impeachment, shall be by jury. . . ."

ARTICLE III OF THE CONSTITUTION

The Constitution guaranteed the right to a trial by jury for anyone who has been accused of committing a crime. The only exception was for impeachment, the charge that a government official had committed a crime. Yet many people believed that the Constitution didn't say enough about what specific rights were included for people who had been accused of crimes. The Sixth Amendment added the specifics:

In all criminal prosecutions, the accused shall enjoy the right to a speedy and public trial, by an impartial jury of the State and district wherein the crime shall have been committed, which districts shall have been previously ascertained by law, and to be informed of the nature and cause of the accusation; to be confronted with the witnesses against him; to have compulsory process for obtaining witnesses in his favor, and to have the assistance of counsel for his defense.

In the new nation, the people of the United States were citizens who owed their loyalty to their government—a government they had created. Under colonial rule, they had been British subjects

William and Mary of England. In 1689, the English Parliament presented these rulers with a declaration that became known as the English Bill of Rights. It established the right to have jurors for trials.

who owed their loyalty to the British monarch, not to elected officials. American citizens did not want their government to become too powerful. Their experiences as British subjects provided reasons for carefully spelling out the details of an accused person's rights at a jury trial. Over the centuries, British subjects had fought for some of these rights and won them. Yet each British monarch had different views of the rights of British subjects. Some of the rights stated in the Sixth Amendment had been sought—but not won—by American colonists when they were still ruled by England.

Many times in English history, English subjects had tried to protect themselves against a despotic, or all-powerful and oppressive, king. The English trace the beginnings of their rights to 1215, when a group of barons met King John in an open field in Runnymede, England. The king wanted two things from the barons: taxes and their oaths of loyalty. The barons were angry because they felt that the king wanted too much from them and didn't offer anything in return. So before they would give the king their money or their loyalty, they drew up a document and demanded that the king sign it and agree to follow its terms. That document is called Magna Carta, or Great Charter. Although Magna Carta was designed to protect the barons, the wording didn't say "barons." It said "free men," and in time, all free Englishmen considered the rights in Magna Carta to belong to all Englishmen.

Magna Carta was an agreement between King John and his barons, not between all English kings and their subjects. Each new monarch was asked to swear to uphold Magna Carta. Over the centuries, however, the Great Charter took on different meanings for the rulers and their subjects. During the seventeenth century, the Stuart kings and Parliament (the lawmaking body in England) had serious disputes. They fought over who had the final word on laws.

In 1621, under the leadership of Sir Edward Coke (pronounced COOK), Parliament drew up a Protestation. In it, the House of Commons spelled out "the ancient and undoubted birthright and inheritance of the subjects of England." They sent it to King James

King John of England signing Magna Carta at Runnymede, 1215.

I, who tore it up and imprisoned Coke and other leaders in the Tower of London.

Charles I, who followed his father to the throne in 1621, believed even more strongly in the rights of the king. He demanded "loans" from his subjects. Those who didn't make the "loans" were sent to prison without a trial, by the king's command. Judges who didn't follow the king's orders were dismissed.

King Charles I of England (painted by Daniel Mytens in 1631). Although he was forced to accept the Petition of Right in 1628, Charles I ruled without Parliament for eleven years. He was condemned as a tyrant and enemy of England and was beheaded in 1649.

Once again, Coke asked Parliament to defend what it understood to be the law of the land. In 1628, Parliament voted the Petition of Right and sent it to Charles I. The Petition indicated the series of laws that established the rights of English subjects. One of these rights was that a subject could not be committed or restrained "for any time or cause whatsoever without showing a cause." Although Charles I disagreed with the Petition, he had to accept it. The king violated the Petition regularly, however, and his judges kept assuring him that he had the right to do so.

Charles I was beheaded in 1649. From then until 1660, England had no monarch. The country was ruled by a republican form of government—that is, a government made up of representatives who were elected by those who could vote. The new government soon became as despotic as the former kings had been. The Stuart kings were returned to the throne in 1660, but James II was forced to flee to France in 1688.

In 1689, the English throne was offered to William and to Mary, the daughter of James II. The condition for accepting the throne was that they would sign the Bill of Rights that Parliament had enacted. This "second Magna Carta," as some call it, established many basic rights. Among them was the right to have jurors for trials. Yet there was no means of enforcing any of the rights spelled out in 1689.

The rights included in the English Bill of Rights were only some of the rights Englishmen enjoyed. Many other rights were included in England's constitution. That constitution is not a single document as is the U.S. Constitution. The English constitution includes many documents, such as Magna Carta and the Bill of Rights. The English constitution also includes common law. Common law is made up of court decisions, customs, and laws created over the centuries. Some were written, and some weren't written—at least not at first.

When the English colonists reached North America, they still considered themselves to be protected by the English constitution, including English common law. Even after the colonies became independent, the new American citizens still believed that they were governed by the rights of Englishmen. Many states wrote these rights into their constitutions, either as separate bills of rights or as parts of the body of the state constitution. Even Vermont, which didn't become the fourteenth state until March 1791, had a constitution that provided for many of these rights. But other states didn't put them in writing.

After studying the proposed U.S. Constitution, which provided for a strong federal government, many citizens of the "several states" became worried. They remembered English history and wanted to have their rights put in writing so they would have a standard that the federal government could meet.

When James Madison began to draft the first amendments to the Constitution, he examined the various state constitutions and documents. He also studied the suggestions that some states had sent in for a bill of rights.

The Sixth Amendment offers protection to people who have been accused of crimes. Like the other amendments in the Bill of Rights, it is based on both the experiences the American colonists had in dealing with England and the experiences of the states. Some of the rights protected by the Sixth Amendment are among the oldest rights of English subjects. Others are new. The new nation was the first in the world to provide such protection for its citizens. Each Sixth Amendment right has its own history and its own reason for being.

Trial by Jury

One of the rights named in Magna Carta is the right to a trial by jury. Although juries as we know them today did not yet exist, the barons at Runnymede believed that allowing a jury of several neighbors to determine a person's guilt or innocence offered more protection than having a king or royal official make such a decision. Trial by jury came to be recognized as one of the oldest rights of English subjects, and Americans wanted to be sure that right would continue. Eleven of the fourteen states (including Vermont) provided for a trial by jury in their constitutions. No other Sixth Amendment right was as widely recognized in state constitutions.

A Speedy Trial

If a person could be arrested and held for years without a trial, the time spent in jail would be punishment for the guilty and the innocent alike. The Virginia Declaration of Rights (1776) was the first written document to assure a speedy trial. By 1791, five states had included the right to a speedy trial in their constitutions.

Although questions still arise about how speedy a speedy trial must be, this requirement places the burden on the government to act as quickly as justice and circumstances permit.

A Public Trial

Americans recognized that secret trials were by their very nature more unfair than public trials. Many governments—both in the past and the present—have found people guilty at secret trials. Secret trials create fear. When the rest of a country doesn't know what is happening, a government can punish those who oppose it by not allowing people to see unfair accusations and punishments. Even a fair secret trial might be considered suspicious because the public didn't know what took place at the trial.

"The traditional Anglo-American distrust for secret trials has been variously ascribed to the notorious use of this practice by the Spanish Inquisition, to the excesses of the English Court of Star Chamber, and to the French monarchy's abuse of the *lettre de cachet* [a sealed letter that sent a person to prison without a trial]," said Justice Hugo Black in 1948. But Black may have been wrong about the Court of Star Chamber, an English court that was abolished in 1641. Even though many Englishmen willingly took their law cases to that court, many people in our time think the Court of Star Chamber is a symbol of unfair, oppressive secret courts.

Western New Jersey was the first place to provide for public trials, and Pennsylvania was the first to include that right in its constitution. But at the time that Madison drafted the Bill of Rights, only Pennsylvania and Vermont had constitutional guarantees for a public trial.

An Impartial Jury

An impartial jury is one that does not take sides or form an opinion before a trial begins. Today we take the idea of an impartial jury for granted, but the earliest English trial juries weren't impartial and they weren't supposed to be. Juries were usually made up of men who lived in the area of the crime and knew the people and the circumstances involved. They were expected to find the defendant guilty. Often they had made up their minds before the trial began.

In modern English law as well as in American law, an accused person is considered, or presumed, innocent unless he or she is proved guilty in a court trial. The prosecutor, the lawyer who works for the government, must prove that the accused person is guilty "beyond a reasonable doubt." Another way of saying this is that the burden of proof belongs to the prosecutor, who must prove that the accused person is guilty. The accused person does not have to prove that he or she is innocent. In many other legal systems, accused people are considered guilty unless they can prove that they are innocent. Because of our presumption of innocence, it is particularly important that a jury be impartial.

A Jury of State and District Wherein the Crime Shall Have Been Committed

When the American colonists first began protesting English laws, many fears and rumors were spread. The colonists worried that they would be shipped to England for trial. In England, they would have little chance of proving their innocence because most of the people who could be helpful were in America.

This part of the Sixth Amendment states that a trial must be held in the "State and district" in which the crime took place. At first Madison used the term *vicinage* (neighborhood) of the crime. After several discussions in Congress, however, he substituted the more specific words "State and district."

The amendment also says, "which districts shall have been previously ascertained [determined] by law." This wording prevents a government from changing a district's boundaries to force a person to be tried in an unfriendly place.

To Be Informed of the Nature and Cause of the Accusation

It seems obvious that a person who is accused of a crime should know what that crime is. Yet throughout history—including our own times—many people around the world have been jailed for years with no specific charges being brought against them. If people don't know the charges against them, they have no way of proving such charges to be untrue or unfair.

Eight states included in their constitutions the right of the accused to be informed of the charges of a crime. Virginia was the first state to do so.

To Confront Witnesses Against Him

When charges are made secretly and the accuser remains anonymous (unnamed or unknown to the accused), spiteful people may accuse those they don't like of wrongdoing. Even honest people may make accusations based on a misunderstanding. The accused needs to have the right to ask questions of the accuser and to challenge incorrect or misleading statements.

The same eight states that provided the right of the accused to know the charges being brought against him or her provided the right to confront witnesses, and Virginia was the first state to provide this right.

Compulsory Process for Obtaining Witnesses in His Favor

The "compulsory process" is known as the subpoena [pronounced suh-PEE-nuh]. A subpoena is a legal order for a person to appear in court and testify. An accused person needs to be able to call upon information from anyone who might help prove his or her innocence. Sometimes people are not willing to go to court. Then the accused needs a way to require them to appear.

New Jersey was the first state to provide this power in its constitution. By 1791, five other states had included it as well.

The Assistance of Counsel

Counsel is usually someone who has been trained in law. In the United States today, that means a lawyer. Because lawyers know what the law is and are also trained to ask the appropriate questions and to protect the accused, lawyers are considered essential to a fair trial.

At the time the Sixth Amendment was written, the English didn't have the right to counsel at a trial, but eight states provided it in their constitutions. New Jersey was the first to do so.

Steps in Criminal Prosecution

The Sixth Amendment concerns criminal cases—cases of people who have been accused of committing a crime. Before a person is accused, the police investigate the crime to find out who committed it. During the investigation, the police may question one or many witnesses (people who saw or heard events that are related to the crime).

At some point the police may decide that a particular person is a suspect, the one they believe committed the crime. The police then try to gather evidence, or proof, that their suspect committed the crime. Evidence may be witnesses' statements or such clues as fingerprints, guns, or letters related to the crime.

The suspect is taken before a judge and arraigned [pronounced uh-RAYND]. This means that the accusations, or charges, against the accused are presented to the judge. The accused person must then answer the charges, usually by saying "guilty" or "not guilty."

In a criminal case in a federal court, the evidence is presented to a grand jury. A grand jury is a group of from twelve to twenty-three citizens whose task is to decide whether there is enough evidence for a trial. (The grand jury doesn't decide whether the accused is guilty or not guilty.) If the grand jury believes there is enough evidence, the suspect is indicted [pronounced in-DITE-ed]. An indictment officially charges a person with committing a crime.

Sometime later, a trial may be held. The accused is now the defendant, a person who must defend himself or herself against the charges. At a trial, the charges and the evidence against the defendant are heard in a court of law by a jury. The official name is a petit [pronounced PET-ee] jury; *petit* means "small." In a criminal court, a jury usually has twelve members, although some states may have as few as six in cases where the death penalty is not a possibility. The prosecutor presents the evidence to the jury, and the defendant's lawyer tries to show that the evidence doesn't prove the defendant is guilty "beyond a reasonable doubt." The judge is in charge. During the trial, the judge may have to decide such questions as whether the law allows certain questions to be asked and whether certain evidence may be presented to the jury.

Witnesses testify at the trial. This means they take an oath, a statement in which they swear to tell the truth. Usually the oath is taken with one hand on the Bible. (Sometimes another religious book or object is used.)

After the members of the jury have heard the evidence, the prosecutor and the defendant's lawyer each make a statement, or summation, to the jury. Then the judge charges the jury by telling them what the law is asking them to decide and what questions they must answer.

After the members of the jury have had a chance to discuss what they heard in court, they give their verdict, or decision. That verdict may be "not guilty." In this case, the defendant is free. Or the jury may convict the defendant by deciding "guilty." A guilty person is given a sentence—usually time spent in jail.

Sometimes members of the jury can't agree on the verdict. (In a federal criminal case, all twelve members of the jury must agree.)

Then a mistrial is declared. The prosecutor may bring a new trial on the same charges with a new jury, or the prosecutor may decide not to bring the defendant to trial again.

A person who has been found guilty has the right to appeal the case if there is reason to believe the trial wasn't fair or if there is new evidence or new witnesses that might prove that the convicted person is not guilty.

Lawsuits, or cases, have names, and many people refer to lawsuits by their names. The names of most lawsuits come from the two parties, or sides, in the lawsuit. The first side named is the party that brings the lawsuit. The second one is the party that is being defended against the suit. The suer sues against, or *versus,* the party who is sued. (*Versus* is abbreviated *v.* or *vs.*) For example, *Marbury* v. *Madison* means that a party named Marbury sued a party named Madison.

Some lawsuits are named in other ways. For example, *in re Oliver* is Latin and means "in the matter of Oliver." *Ex parte Milligan* is also Latin. It means "on the side of Milligan."

The Bill of Rights states what people's rights are, but not how those rights would be protected. Eventually that question was answered by the Supreme Court under John Marshall, who was chief justice from 1801 to 1835. During that time, Marshall and his associate justices developed and strengthened the concept of judicial review. *Judicial review* means the power of the Supreme Court to decide whether laws, official actions based on laws, and other actions by public officials violate the U.S. Constitution. Because the Constitution is the basic law of the land, the laws and actions of different states are not supposed to conflict with it. Judicial review in the United States takes place when a lawsuit is brought to the Supreme Court.

Most historians agree that the Bill of Rights was written to protect American citizens from abuses by the federal government. Each state also provided its own set of rights, but most states didn't include the entire group of rights provided by the federal government. For example, one state provided the right of trial by jury and

Chief Justice John Marshall served on the Supreme Court from 1801 to 1835. He was one of the main founders of the American system of constitutional law, including the practice of judicial review. He wrote the majority opinion in *Barron* v. *Baltimore* (1833), which stated that the Bill of Rights protected citizens against actions of the *federal government,* not those of state or local governments.

the right to a public trial. Another didn't guarantee the right to a public trial but did guarantee the right to subpoena witnesses. No state adopted the entire federal Bill of Rights into its constitution. As new states entered the Union, each provided its own group of rights. As a result, people in different states had different rights.

When he first proposed the Bill of Rights, James Madison suggested an amendment that said: "No State shall infringe [violate] the equal rights of conscience, nor the freedom of speech, or of the press, or of the right of trial by jury in criminal cases." But that suggestion was rejected before it could go to the different states for a vote.

Apparently the Bill of Rights protected citizens and the states against the federal government, but it didn't protect citizens from the actions of their state governments. Or did it?

One citizen tested this question in 1833. John Barron asked the Supreme Court to declare that a clause, or phrase, of the Fifth Amendment of the Bill of Rights protected him from actions taken by the city of Baltimore. That Fifth Amendment clause says "nor shall private property be taken for public use, without just compensation [payment]."

John Barron owned and operated a wharf in water that was deep enough to allow ships to dock in the Baltimore Harbor. The city of Baltimore paved some streets and caused a few streams to flow in a different direction. After this work, the water at Barron's wharf was just a small, shallow inlet, and ships could no longer dock there. Barron lost a lot of income because of these public improvements. He thought that the city of Baltimore had taken his property (the deep wharf) and changed it for public use (creating new streets) without paying him for his loss.

After appealing to Maryland state courts and losing, Barron appealed his case to the U.S. Supreme Court. The Supreme Court, in *Barron* v. *Baltimore* (1833), declared that the Fifth Amendment did not apply to the states. This meant that the Supreme Court had no jurisdiction (authority to decide) in Barron's case.

That seemed to settle matters for the entire Bill of Rights. The Supreme Court had decided that the federal Bill of Rights applied only to acts of the federal government. It did not apply to actions by state or local governments. That decision remained in effect for more than ninety years.

CHAPTER 2

The Fourteenth Amendment— A "Second Bill of Rights"?

"We are under a Constitution, but the Constitution is what the judges say it is."

CHARLES EVANS HUGHES

From 1861 to 1865, the United States was torn by the Civil War. After it ended, the nation passed the Thirteenth Amendment—in 1865—which outlawed slavery. But outlawing slavery didn't fully address the problem of the status of these new "freemen," as the freed men, women, and children were called. Were they full citizens? What rights did they have?

The Constitution (Article I, Section 8) gives Congress the power "[t]o establish a uniform rule of naturalization. . . ." *Naturalization* means granting citizenship to people who weren't born in the United States. The former slaves, however, *were* born in the United States. Yet most states didn't consider them to be citizens with full rights to vote, serve on juries, and so forth.

The Fourteenth Amendment, which was ratified in 1868, dealt with these issues. The Fourteenth Amendment has five sections. Sections 2, 3, and 4 deal with matters that concerned former Confederate soldiers, officials, and Confederate war debts. Sections 1 and 5 have a much broader application.

Associate Justice Benjamin N. Cardozo served on the Supreme Court from 1932 to 1938. According to Cardozo, some rights must definitely be guaranteed against actions by the states. These "fundamental rights" included "freedom of thought and freedom of speech."

Section 1. All persons born or naturalized in the United States, and subject to the jurisdiction thereof, are citizens of the United States and of the State wherein they reside. No State shall make or enforce any law which shall abridge [shorten or restrict] the privileges or immunities [protections] of citizens of the United States; nor shall any State deprive any person of life, liberty, or property, without due process of law; nor deny to any person within its jurisdiction the equal protection of the laws.

Section 5. The Congress shall have power to enforce, by appropriate legislation, the provisions of this article.

What did the Fourteenth Amendment do? Did it (as some experts believe) make the entire Bill of Rights binding on the states as well as on the federal government? Is that why the phrase "privileges or immunities" was used? Is that why the wording "deprive any person of life, liberty, or property, without due process of law" sounds so much like the wording used in the Fifth Amendment? Does "the equal protection of the laws" mean protection of citizens' rights against actions by the states as well as actions by the federal government?

Did the Fourteenth Amendment intend to make the federal Bill of Rights apply to the states? If so, did the entire Bill of Rights apply to the states or did just some parts of the Bill of Rights apply to the states? For more than a hundred years, legal experts have argued about these questions.

The term *incorporation* is often used to refer to the idea that the Fourteenth Amendment makes the Bill of Rights apply to the "several states." Sometimes people talk of the "nationalization" of the Bill of Rights, of its "absorption," or of "carrying it over" to apply to the states. These words don't have exactly the same meanings. But they all suggest that the states as well as the federal government are constitutionally required to respect the rights protected by the Bill of Rights. If that is what the Fourteenth Amendment really means, it becomes "a second Bill of Rights."

Many people pointed out that the United States has a federal system. Under the federal system, most powers or responsibilities belong either to the federal government or to the state governments. (A few responsibilities are shared.) The federal government is responsible for laws that govern the nation, while each state government is responsible for its own laws. Many people worried that incorporation of the federal Bill of Rights would destroy the federal system by taking too much power and responsibility away from the states.

The first important Supreme Court case to raise the issue of incorporation came in 1873. Like the earlier case of *Barron* v. *Baltimore* (1833), this lawsuit had to do with property rights. The case is often called the *Slaughterhouse* cases because it concerned a Louisiana law involving butchers. The Louisiana legislature had given one livestock slaughtering company a monopoly (total control) of the butcher business in the area around New Orleans. This deprived all the other butchers in the area of their livelihood (the means by which they earned their living). A group of these out-of-work butchers filed lawsuits claiming that Louisiana had abridged the "privileges or immunities" of citizens of the United States. The butchers also claimed that they had a right to the equal protection of the laws.

The Supreme Court didn't agree. The majority—more than half—of the justices (five) believed that the Fourteenth Amendment was intended to be mainly applied only to the civil rights of African Americans. In deciding the *Slaughterhouse* cases, the Court had an early opportunity to say that—even after the Fourteenth Amendment was passed—the federal Bill of Rights did not apply to the states. The majority opinion declared that there were two kinds of citizenship, or "dual citizenship." One was citizenship in a state. People became citizens of a state simply by living in that state. The other was national citizenship. People became citizens of the nation either by birth or by naturalization. The majority opinion stated that the Fourteenth Amendment's "privileges and immunities" clause could be used only to forbid states from interfering with the rights of national citizenship, not with the rights of state citizenship.

Did the *Slaughterhouse* decision mean that none of the protections granted by the Bill of Rights would be incorporated by the Fourteenth Amendment? The next important case to try to test this question was *Hurtado* v. *California* (1884). This case involved the rights of a person in a murder trial.

Joseph Hurtado was accused of committing a murder in California. He was convicted and sentenced to be hanged. He appealed his conviction, claiming that he had been denied the "due process" provided for in the Fourteenth Amendment because he had not been indicted by a grand jury. Instead of a grand jury indictment, the prosecutor had prepared an information (a list of charges) against Hurtado.

The Fifth Amendment clearly states that "[n]o person shall be held to answer for a capital, or otherwise infamous crime, unless on a presentment or indictment [formal charges] of a Grand Jury. . . ." A capital crime is one in which the accused can be given the death sentence if he or she is found guilty. The use of an information instead of a grand jury was legal in some states, but usually only for lesser crimes. English common law limited the use of an information to misdemeanors (lesser crimes). Murder is a felony (serious crime). Could a person be found guilty of a capital crime in a state court if he or she had not been indicted by a grand jury?

The Supreme Court decided by a vote of 7 to 1 that the grand jury is not essential to due process. Justice Stanley Matthews wrote the majority opinion. In it he stated that due process need not be limited to one kind of procedure. He said:

> [A] process of law, which is not otherwise forbidden, must be taken to be due process of law, if it can show the sanction [official approval] of settled usage both in England and in this country; but it by no means follows that nothing else can be due process of law.

The only person who opposed this decision was Justice John Marshall Harlan. In later cases, Harlan would remain the main

Associate Justice John Marshall Harlan I served on the Supreme Court from 1877 to 1911. He often dissented from the majority opinions of his time. Harlan wanted the rights in the Bill of Rights to be safeguarded from state actions, not just from those of the federal government.

voice in favor of incorporation, even when the majority declared against it. Harlan served from 1877 to 1911. (In 1955 his grandson, John Marshall Harlan II, became a Supreme Court justice. The younger Harlan usually opposed incorporation, however, and was the main voice against it. The younger Harlan believed that there were other ways of extending the protections of the Bill of Rights without using direct incorporation.)

In the argument he gave in the *Hurtado* case, the first Justice Harlan asked:

> Does not the fact that the people of the original States required an amendment of the National Constitution, securing exemption from prosecution, for a capital offense, except upon the indictment or presentment of a grand jury, prove that, in their judgment, such an exemption was essential to protection against accusation and un-founded prosecution, and therefore, was a fundamental principle in liberty and justice?

The decision in the *Hurtado* case was clear. The Court did not accept the idea of incorporation.

In 1900, Charles Maxwell again raised the question of due process when he was brought to trial in Utah on an information instead of a grand-jury indictment. In this case, however, there was another issue. It involved the Sixth Amendment. Maxwell was convicted by a jury of eight people, not the usual twelve. The case of *Maxwell* v. *Dow* (1900) raised two issues. Had the due process clause of the Fifth Amendment been violated because Maxwell was not indicted by a grand jury? Had the Sixth Amendment right to a trial by an impartial jury been violated because Maxwell's jury had only eight members?

The justices relied on the precedent (earlier decision) they had established in the *Hurtado* case. They decided against Maxwell and against incorporation of the Fifth and Sixth Amendment rights. They ruled that a state may use an eight-person jury instead of the twelve jurors required in federal court. Once again, Justice Harlan provided the only voice of dissent, or disagreement.

In 1908, the Supreme Court again decided against the incorporation of a Fifth Amendment right. The clause in the Fifth Amendment says that a person shall not "be compelled [forced] in any criminal case to be a witness against himself. . . ." This is called protection against self-incrimination (being forced to give evidence damaging to oneself such as evidence showing that one has committed a crime). The case *Twining* v. *New Jersey* (1908) involved the right not to be forced to incriminate oneself. The *Twining* decision, however, provided a new standard by which due process might mean that some Bill of Rights assurances would be protected from state action. It involved "inalienable rights," those rights that cannot be given up or taken away. In writing the decision, Justice William Moody asked this question: "Is it a fundamental principle in liberty and justice which inheres in [is essential to] the very idea of a free government and is the inalienable right of a citizen of such a government?"

As in the two earlier incorporation cases—*Hurtado* v. *California* (1884) and *Maxwell* v. *Dow* (1900)—Justice Harlan dissented. He continued to believe that the Fourteenth Amendment incorporated the entire Bill of Rights. Up to this time, only one of the Bill of Rights guarantees (the right to just compensation if property is taken for public use) had been incorporated through the Fourteenth Amendment.

During the early twentieth century, new justices joined the Court, and some of them were more inclined to favor the concept of incorporation. The first sign of change came in the case of *Gitlow* v. *New York* (1925). It involved the First Amendment rights of free speech and free press.

Benjamin Gitlow was an extremely radical left-wing Socialist. He often spoke and wrote advocating, or supporting, the overthrow of the U.S. government. In doing so, he violated a New York State law on criminal anarchy. This means that he encouraged the overthrow of the government by violent means. Gitlow was tried in New York and found guilty of advocating the overthrow of organized government by violence. He kept appealing his conviction in the New York State courts, and he kept losing. In 1925, he took his case to the Supreme Court. His argument was that the state's law on

Benjamin Gitlow's case was appealed to the Supreme Court. The Court upheld his conviction, but its opinion mentioned that freedom of speech and freedom of the press were rights protected from state actions.

criminal anarchy violated both the freedom of speech guarantees of the First Amendment and the due process clause of the Fourteenth Amendment. Gitlow lost his case, but a small victory was achieved for incorporation.

The Supreme Court upheld the state law under which Gitlow had been found guilty of "direct incitement" (actions that would not be protected by the First Amendment). But it agreed that the due process clause of the Fourteenth Amendment does protect freedom of speech and freedom of the press:

> For present purposes we may and do assume that freedom of speech and of the press—which are protected by the First Amendment from abridgement [being weakened or taken away] by Congress—are among the fundamental personal rights and "liberties" protected by the due process clause of the Fourteenth Amendment from impairment [damage or weakening] by the States.

Two justices, Oliver Wendell Holmes and Louis D. Brandeis, agreed with that statement. But they didn't believe that Gitlow's words or writings provided a "clear and present danger" to the state. They felt his rights of speech and press should have been protected. Nevertheless, it appeared that the Supreme Court might be considering the incorporation of some federal Bill of Rights protections.

In 1925 and 1927, two court cases clearly established the idea that freedom of speech was considered to be protected against state actions. Freedom of speech was the first right to be incorporated. In 1931, freedom of the press was also recognized as an incorporated right. Incorporation apparently would have to be gained one right at a time.

The Sixth Amendment right to counsel became an issue in an event that had hit the front pages of most of the nation's newspapers. Nine poor, uneducated young African Americans, ranging in age from twelve to twenty, were pulled off a freight train near Scottsboro, Alabama, and arrested. The authorities there were alerted by some white boys who had fought with the black boys and had been thrown off the train.

The nine young blacks were accused of raping two white girls on the train. If the nine were found guilty, the punishment would be death. Four of them were traveling together from Chattanooga, Tennessee. Two of these four—Roy and Andrew Wright—were brothers. The other five were from Georgia but didn't seem to know one another.

A mob gathered outside the jail. They threatened to lynch (hang without a trial) the young African Americans, but the judge was determined to try the boys in court. He was sure they would be found guilty, and the town would look more civilized if the accused were executed with due process.

The accused couldn't afford to pay a lawyer, so the judge declared that all seven of Scottsboro's lawyers would represent them at the arraignment. (In an arraignment, the accused is brought

The "Scottsboro boys" being guarded by the Alabama National Guard, 1931. Angry mobs had threatened to lynch the prisoners. Their trials led to two major Supreme Court decisions.

before a judge to answer the charges against him or her.) All except one of the lawyers excused themselves. The lawyer who represented the accused for the arraignment didn't talk to them at first.

At the trials, this lawyer and another were in court, but neither of them would claim to represent the defendants. One said he was there at the request of "people who are interested in them." (The people were members of a church group in Chattanooga.) The defendants didn't have time to prepare a defense with the lawyers who were present but were not really representing them.

Meanwhile, an angry mob of whites had gathered in the streets. Eight of the boys were tried hastily in four groups by four different juries. The main witness against them was one of the women who claimed to have been raped. She kept contradicting herself in her testimony. The testimony of several of the other witnesses was also confusing.

While the second trial was in progress, the jury heard cheers from the crowd as the first jury's verdict was heard. The first two defendants had been found guilty and were sentenced to death. The third defendant was also found guilty and sentenced to death. At the third trial, there were five defendants. They, too, were found guilty. At the last trial, of thirteen-year-old Roy Wright, the prosecutor asked for life imprisonment, but seven jurors wanted to sentence him to death. The case ended in a mistrial.

After the defendants had been convicted, various groups around the country began talking about new trials and freeing the "Scottsboro boys" (as they were called). Some described the trials as "legal lynching." After appeals through the Alabama courts, the case reached the Supreme Court as *Powell* v. *Alabama* (1932). The main question in that case was whether the Sixth Amendment right to counsel under federal law also applied to the states through the due process clause of the Fourteenth Amendment.

The Supreme Court decided in favor of the defendants. The Court decided that they had been denied the right of counsel and the customary opportunity to prepare for a trial. In other words, the state had violated the right to counsel guaranteed by the Sixth Amendment through the due process clause of the Fourteenth Amendment.

The defendants weren't set free at that time. The death penalty was still a very real possibility for them. They would go on to defend themselves at further trials and another Supreme Court case involving incorporation.

Did the *Powell* v. *Alabama* (1932) decision mean that the Sixth Amendment right to counsel had now been incorporated? Did states have to provide lawyers for those who could not afford to pay their fees? At first it seemed so. Then the Court stated that the states had to provide counsel *only* in capital cases, cases involving serious crimes that might lead to the death penalty.

Other Supreme Court decisions handed down during the 1930s made almost the entire First Amendment binding upon the states. These rights included the rights to freedom of speech, press, religion, assembly and petition.

The issue of incorporation was addressed again in a decision handed down in 1937. *Palko* v. *Connecticut* (1937) involved a case that was related to the Fifth Amendment clause "nor shall any person be subject for the same offense to be twice put in jeopardy of life or limb. . . ."

Many states have different levels of murder. Conviction for murder in the first degree is more severe than it is for murder in the second degree. People who have been convicted of first-degree murder usually receive heavier sentences than those who have been convicted of second-degree murder.

Frank Palko had been tried in Connecticut for murder in the first degree for killing two police officers, but the trial jury found him guilty of murder in the second degree. Instead of accepting that verdict, the state asked for and received a new trial. This time Palko was found guilty of murder in the first degree and was sentenced to death. He appealed the verdict. The argument used in his appeal was that "whatever is forbidden by the Fifth Amendment is forbidden by the Fourteenth also." Double jeopardy was forbidden by the Fifth Amendment. (The term *double jeopardy* means standing trial for the same crime for which you have already been tried and received a verdict.) The Supreme Court denied Palko's appeal, and he was executed.

Justice Benjamin Cardozo wrote the majority opinion. In it he discussed the entire question of whether the Fourteenth Amendment made the Bill of Rights constitutional law for the states as well as for the federal government. Cardozo declared that there was no general rule incorporating the entire Bill of Rights. He noted that the defendant claimed:

[T]he Fourteenth Amendment is to be taken as embodying the prohibitions of the Fifth. His thesis is even broader. Whatever would be a violation of the original bill of rights (Amendments 1 to 8) if done by the federal government is now equally unlawful by force of the Fourteenth Amendment if done by a state. There is no such general rule.

"There is no such general rule." That was the fullest statement the Court had made so far. Some rights, Cardozo's opinion noted, had been incorporated. These were what Cardozo called "fundamental" rights. Among these were freedom of thought and of speech. Other rights, he claimed, were formal, not fundamental, and formal rights were not incorporated. Among the list of non-incorporated formal rights were trial by jury, grand-jury indictment for a "capital or other infamous crime," protection from self-incrimination, and protection from double jeopardy.

The idea behind formal rights is that some rights can be assured in different forms. The fact that the form is different doesn't mean that the right is lost.

The Fourteenth Amendment, ratified in 1868, was nearly seventy years old at the time of the *Palko* decision. During those seventy years, only the First Amendment rights had become almost fully incorporated. One Sixth Amendment right, the right to counsel in criminal cases (but only if they were capital cases), had been accepted as "fundamental" and "implicit [understood] in the concept of ordered liberty. . . ."

The *Palko* decision made the Court's position clear: The Fourteenth Amendment had not incorporated the entire Bill of Rights.

The Right to Counsel

"Social order is based on law, and its perpetuity [continuing existence] on fair and impartial administration."

JUDGE JAMES EDWIN HORTON, JR.

The *Palko* (1937) decision stated that the Bill of Rights had not been totally incorporated by the Fourteenth Amendment. If it had been entirely incorporated, the whole Bill of Rights would apply to the states. The *Palko* decision meant that each right would have to be fought for separately. Amendments like the Sixth had several clauses, each for separate rights. Each specific right would have to be argued in the highest court. Sometimes the issue would have to be decided several times in different situations. That is exactly what happened with claims for the right to counsel.

Although the right to counsel in criminal cases was specifically mentioned in the Sixth Amendment, the wording didn't say whether that right belonged only to people who wanted a lawyer and could afford to pay the fee. In 1938, the Supreme Court had to decide that question for federal cases. In *Johnson* v. *Zerbst* (1938), the Court decided that lawyers had to be provided for defendants in federal criminal cases.

What about cases in state courts and poor defendants who were on trial? Were they also entitled to counsel?

This law-enforcement officer is reading the Miranda warnings, which tell a person suspected of a crime what his or her rights are.

Smith Betts thought they were. At least he thought that he was entitled to counsel when he was charged with robbery in Carroll County, Maryland. Betts asked the Maryland court to appoint a lawyer because he couldn't afford to hire one. The judge refused, saying that the court appointed lawyers only in cases involving murder and rape. So Betts, who was a poor, unemployed, barely educated farmhand, acted as his own lawyer. After his conviction, Betts appealed to the Maryland courts. He argued that his constitutional right to counsel had been denied. The Maryland judge said that Betts's trial was simple and the defendant was able "to take care of his own interests."

The Supreme Court considered *Betts* v. *Brady* in 1942. Many people expected the Court to decide in favor of Betts. After all, the *Palko* decision had said that the due process clause of the Fourteenth Amendment "may make it unlawful for a state to abridge by its statutes" freedom of speech, freedom of the press, the free exercise of religion, the right of peaceable assembly,

> . . . or the right of one accused of crime to the benefit of counsel. . . . In these and other situations immunities [protections] that are valid as against the federal government . . . have been found to be implicit [understood] in the concept of ordered liberty, and thus, through the Fourteenth Amendment, become valid as against the states.

Yet the Court had said that the *Powell* v. *Alabama* (1932) decision applied only to capital crimes and had decided, 6 to 3, that Betts wasn't entitled to court-ordered counsel. Justice Owen Roberts wrote the majority opinion. He stated that the American right to counsel was intended to permit a defendant to have counsel, not to require a state to provide it. The right to counsel "is not a fundamental right, essential to a fair trial." Nevertheless, a state should provide counsel when there were "special" or "exceptional" circumstances—such as mental illness, youth, lack of education, illiteracy, and so forth.

Justices Hugo Black, William Douglas, and Frank Murphy dissented. Black wrote the dissenting opinion. In it he stated his belief that the Fourteenth Amendment had intended to incorporate the Sixth Amendment. He quoted from an 1854 Indiana Supreme Court opinion:

It is not to be thought of, in a civilized community, for a moment that any citizen put in jeopardy of [danger of losing] life or liberty, should be debarred of [denied] counsel because he was too poor to employ such aid. No court could be respected, or respect itself, to sit and hear such a trial.

The *Betts* decision was made during World War II, a war that most Americans believed was being fought to preserve democracy and fundamental rights. Noted lawyers wrote letters and articles objecting to the *Betts* v. *Brady* (1942) decision, especially at that time in history. One letter to the *New York Times* said:

Throughout the world men are fighting to be free from the fear of political trials and concentration camps. From this struggle men are hoping that a bill of rights will emerge which will guarantee to all men certain fundamental rights. . . . Most Americans—lawyers and laymen [nonlawyers] alike—before the decision in *Betts* v. *Brady* would have thought that the right of the accused to counsel in a serious criminal case was unquestionably a part of our own Bill of Rights.

Applying the "special" or "exceptional" circumstances that the *Betts* decision required became very complicated. Many convicted prisoners petitioned the Supreme Court to review their cases because special circumstances entitled them to a lawyer. The Court found itself granting many petitions for counsel. The decision in *Betts* v. *Brady* was becoming very difficult to put into practice, and several justices wanted to see it overturned. (When the justices change an earlier decision, they are said to *overturn* the decision.)

Clarence Earl Gideon provided the Supreme Court with an opportunity to reexamine the *Betts* v. *Brady* (1942) decision. In 1961, Gideon was arrested in Panama City, Florida, for breaking and entering a pool hall with the intent to commit petty larceny (minor theft). When the judge at the trial asked Gideon if he was ready for trial, he said he wasn't ready because he had no counsel. Then he said, "I request this Court to appoint counsel to represent me in this trial."

The judge said that he could not appoint counsel for Gideon. "Under the laws of the State of Florida," he said, "the only time the court can appoint counsel to represent a Defendant is when that person is charged with a capital offense. I am sorry, but I will have to deny your request to appoint counsel to defend you in this case."

Gideon answered, "The United States Supreme Court says I am entitled to be represented by counsel."

Both the judge and Gideon were mistaken. Florida allowed judges to appoint counsel anytime they thought it was necessary, but judges *had to* provide counsel only in capital cases. At the time of Gideon's trial in Panama City, three large Florida cities had supplied counsel to many defendants in criminal cases, but Gideon's judge may not have known that. Gideon was mistaken because the Supreme Court had *not* ruled that he was entitled to counsel.

Although Gideon did his best to act as his own lawyer, he was convicted and was sentenced to jail for five years. From jail, he sent a writ of habeas corpus to the Florida Supreme Court claiming that he had been imprisoned illegally. A writ of habeas corpus is an order to bring a person before a judge to see whether he or she is being held for a good reason. If no such reason is found, the person may be set free. Gideon's request for a writ of habeas corpus was denied.

Gideon then sat down with a pencil and prison stationery and wrote a petition to the U.S. Supreme Court *in forma pauperis* ("in the manner of a pauper"—a very poor person). In the petition, he asked that his case be reviewed. The motion *in forma pauperis* meant that if the Court accepted the case, Gideon wouldn't have to

Clarence Gideon. In *Gideon* v. *Wainwright* (1963), the Supreme Court ruled that in cases involving serious crimes "those too poor to hire a lawyer... cannot be assured a fair trial unless counsel is provided for them." The Sixth Amendment right to counsel therefore applies to state criminal trials as well as federal ones.

pay the costs for supplying documents. The Court would appoint a lawyer to represent him.

The Supreme Court usually does not like to overturn its earlier decisions. The Court also tries to respect the division of authority between the states and the federal government whenever possible. So many people were surprised when the Court accepted Gideon's appeal. Was the 1942 *Betts* v. *Brady* decision—made only twenty-one years earlier—going to be overturned?

Abe Fortas, who later became a Supreme Court justice, was appointed to represent Gideon. Fortas decided not to argue that the Fourteenth Amendment incorporated the Sixth Amendment. Instead, he claimed that the right to counsel is a fundamental right that is a necessary part of a fair trial. Fortas showed that most of the states agreed. In 1962, thirty-seven of the fifty states provided counsel in all felony cases. Eight more states usually provided counsel. That left only five states that provided counsel only in capital cases. Florida was one of them.

The Supreme Court decided unanimously (all the justices agreed) in favor of Gideon. Justice Hugo Black (who had written the dissenting opinion in the *Betts* v. *Brady* case) wrote the opinion in *Gideon* v. *Wainright* (1963). He recognized that the question before the Court in the *Gideon* case was, "Should this Court's holding in *Betts* v. *Brady* be reconsidered?" Black declared:

> [I]n our adversary system of criminal justice, any person haled [forced] into court, who is too poor to hire a lawyer, cannot be assured a fair trial unless counsel is provided for him. This seems to us to be an obvious truth. Governments, both state and federal, quite properly spend vast sums of money to establish machinery to try defendants accused of crime. Lawyers to prosecute are everywhere deemed essential [believed to be absolutely necessary] to protect the public's interest in an orderly society. Similarly, there are few defendants charged with crime, few indeed, who fail to hire the best lawyers they can get to prepare and present their defenses. . . . The right of one charged with crime to counsel may not be deemed fundamental and essential for fair trials in some countries, but it is in ours.

The *Gideon* decision incorporated a defendant's right to have a lawyer's help in preparing for and conducting a trial. But what about the rights of an accused person when he or she is first arrested? That question reached the Court the following year.

Danny Escobedo was arrested for murder in Illinois and interrogated, or questioned. During the police interrogation, Escobedo kept asking to see his lawyer. But he was continually refused. At the same time, Escobedo's lawyer repeatedly requested permission to see him. The lawyer's request was also denied. The police didn't tell Escobedo that he had the right to remain silent—a right his lawyer might have explained. At Escobedo's trial, statements he had made during questioning were used against him. As a result, he was found guilty of murder.

Escobedo's 1964 appeal to the Supreme Court centered on his Sixth Amendment right to counsel and his Fifth Amendment right to remain silent. The police didn't honor either of these rights during the questioning. Therefore, Escobedo claimed, the trial wasn't fair and impartial.

In a 5 to 4 decision in *Escobedo* v. *Illinois* (1964), the Court agreed with Escobedo and overturned his conviction. Justice Arthur Goldberg wrote the majority opinion and spoke of a person's constitutional rights: "No system worth preserving should have to *fear* that if an accused is permitted to consult with a lawyer, he will become aware of and exercise these rights."

Justice Byron White wrote the dissent. He felt that it would now be more difficult to convict a person because it would be almost impossible to interrogate a suspect. White argued:

> The right to counsel now not only entitles the accused to counsel's advice and aid in preparing for a trial, but stands as an impenetrable barrier to any interrogation once the accused has become a suspect.

The *Escobedo* decision extended the incorporation of the right to counsel to the time at which a person first becomes a suspect. Although the police may question many people in a general investigation, once a person becomes a suspect, he or she is entitled to counsel. But how could a suspect be told of the right to counsel?

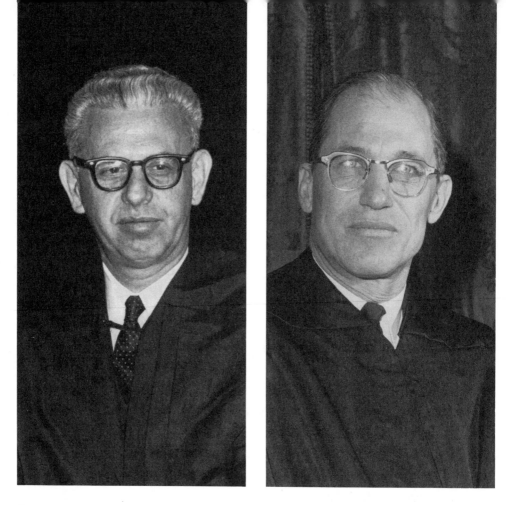

Associate Justice Arthur J. Goldberg (left) wrote the majority opinion in *Escobedo* v. *Illinois* (1964): A confession of a suspect held by law-enforcement officials could not be used if the suspect had asked for and was refused a lawyer and if he or she had not been warned of the right to remain silent. Associate Justice Byron R. White (right) dissented. He believed that the Supreme Court decision would make the police officer's job of questioning suspects very difficult.

Anybody who watches police movies has heard of the Miranda warning. A Miranda warning tells a person suspected of a crime what his or her rights are. Different cities and states use different wording, but most Miranda warnings say something like this:

1. You have the right to remain silent and refuse to answer questions.
2. Anything you do say may be used against you in a court of law.

3. You have the right to consult an attorney before speaking to the police and to have an attorney present during any questioning now or in the future.
4. If you cannot afford an attorney, one will be provided for you without cost.
5. If you do not have an attorney available, you have the right to remain silent until you have had an opportunity to consult with one.
6. Now that I have advised you of your rights, are you willing to answer questions without an attorney present?

The suspect must say that he or she understands each right. Some parts of the warning refer to Fifth Amendment rights to keep silent and avoid incriminating oneself. Others tell the suspect about the Sixth Amendment right to counsel. These warnings are supposed to be given before a *suspect* is questioned. If a person is questioned about a crime but isn't a suspect, the police don't give the warning. The warning is given when "the investigation is no longer a general inquiry into an unsolved crime but has begun to focus on a particular suspect."

The *Miranda* v. *Arizona* (1966) decision came about because Ernesto Miranda, a twenty-one-year-old truck driver in Phoenix, Arizona, was arrested and convicted for kidnapping and raping an eighteen-year-old girl. The girl identified him in a lineup. (A lineup allows a witness to identify the suspect when he or she is standing with a group of others.) The police interrogated Miranda, and at the end of two hours, he confessed to having committed the crime. Miranda signed the confession, which also stated that he had signed willingly. Miranda's lawyer objected to having the confession, which had been made without the presence of a lawyer, read at the trial. But it was allowed as part of the evidence, and Miranda was convicted. Miranda's appeal was based on the absence of a lawyer at the time of questioning.

The Supreme Court ruled 5 to 4 in favor of Ernesto Miranda. The effect of the *Miranda* decision was that the police could no

Ernesto Miranda (right) just before he was convicted for a second time on the charge of kidnap and rape. His first conviction had been reversed by the Supreme Court in 1966.

longer question a suspect in custody without the suspect's consent unless an attorney was present. Chief Justice Earl Warren wrote the majority decision and noted: "The cases before us raise questions which go to the very root of our concepts of American criminal jurisprudence [system of laws]."

Three of the four dissenting justices disagreed very strongly with the decision and spoke out against it. They said that it was a dangerous thing to do at a time when the crime rate was growing and many people were worried about crime. Together with many police officers and prosecutors, the dissenting justices worried that the decision was placing "a balance in favor of the accused."

In a dissent to *Miranda,* Justice John Marshall Harlan wrote:

The new rules are not designed to guard against police brutality or other unmistakable banned forms of coercion [force]. . . . Rather the thrust of the new rules is to negate [undo] all pressures, to reinforce the nervous or ignorant suspect, and ultimately to discourage any confession at all.

Ernesto Miranda was tried again on the same charge of kidnap and rape, and the courts used other evidence to convict him. He went to prison but was paroled (released before he had completed his sentence). Then he was tried and imprisoned for another crime and paroled again. He was killed in a barroom fight in 1976. In a twist of fate, when the suspect in Miranda's murder was arrested, the police used a Miranda warning to advise him of his rights.

When the public sees that court decisions protect criminals as well as innocent people, many people grow angry. They call for more "law and order." That often means fewer rules that interfere with the right of the police to question suspects. Most law-enforcement officials object to having restrictions placed on them when they try to solve crimes. On the other hand, a suspect might be encouraged, tricked, or forced to say more when a lawyer isn't present to advise silence. Many people have been tried and convicted chiefly because they confessed to crimes, sometimes to crimes they didn't commit. The Miranda rule doesn't make it impossible for police to solve crimes or for suspects to confess. But it does require the police to work harder at investigating a crime. Often the police uncover very convincing evidence. Then no confession is necessary. At other times, without a confession the police have no way to bring a suspect to court.

Those who approve of the *Miranda* decision point out that innocent people have confessed to crimes because of psychological—and sometimes physical—effects of a long police interrogation.

Justice William O. Douglas wrote:

The rights of those accused of crime are important because people may be and often are falsely accused. One judge recently concluded, after observing criminal trials for two or more decades, that

The Warren Court, mid-1960s. The justices reached a large number of decisions that required the states to respect the rights in the Bill of Rights.

more innocent men have probably been convicted than guilty men permitted to go free. The safeguards built into every trial are designed to protect against such miscarriages of justice. . . . In short, the liberties of none are safe unless the liberties of all are protected.

As a result of the *Miranda* decision, those who are arrested must be told that they have a right to counsel. Even so, suspects often find themselves in circumstances where they can't speak to their lawyers. In 1976, the Supreme Court found that a defendant shouldn't have been prevented from consulting his lawyer during an overnight break while still testifying. In another case, the Court found that police officers had interfered with a defendant while driving him to the place of trial. This was done even though the officers had promised the defendant's lawyer that they wouldn't question him during the drive.

At first the right to court-appointed counsel applied only to suspects on trial for "nonpetty offenses punishable by more than six months imprisonment." But in 1972, in *Argersinger* v. *Hamlin,* the Supreme Court ruled on a case in which a poor defendant had had no counsel when he was tried by a judge for carrying a gun. The maximum sentence would have been six months and a fine of $1,000. The judge sentenced the defendant to ninety days. In reviewing the case, the Supreme Court said that the Sixth Amendment applied to "all criminal prosecutions" and the defendant was entitled to counsel. The Court made an exception for traffic court and a few petty, or minor, offenses that didn't involve jail.

By the mid-1970s, almost all defendants—rich or poor—had the right to be represented by counsel in criminal cases. They also gained the right to have counsel at parole hearings and at hearings to decide if they should be committed to a mental hospital.

In 1984 and 1985, the Court ruled on *effective* counsel when it stated that a convicted person may appeal a conviction because of poor representation. But "poor representation" must be proved. A new counsel and trial are granted only when there is a reasonable chance of changing the result in a new trial.

The Supreme Court also ruled that a defendant has the right to refuse counsel and represent himself or herself. When that happens, a "standby counsel" may be ordered by the court to provide assistance.

CHAPTER

4

The Right to a Speedy and Public Trial

"The history of liberty has largely been the history of observance of
procedural safeguards."

McNabb v. *United States* (1943)

While the Sixth Amendment grants the right to a speedy and
public trial, it doesn't define "speedy" or "public." These guarantees are for the person who has been accused of a crime. Sometimes
the problem is that a trial is too speedy or too public.

A Speedy Trial

A "speedy trial" may be the most difficult part of the Sixth
Amendment to define. To protect the rights of both the accused and
the public, a trial should take place as soon as possible after
someone has been accused of a crime. But both the defendant and
the prosecutor need time to prepare for a trial. Many circumstances
may get in the way of a speedy trial. Among them are a crowded
court schedule and the availability of witnesses. In addition,
continuances, or postponements, may be requested by either the
prosecutor or the defense.

Often the defendant is not eager for a speedy trial, especially if
he or she is not in jail while awaiting trial. Whenever a trial is
delayed, witnesses may move away or die, or they may forget

After 1967, states could no longer legally deny people the Sixth Amendment
right to a speedy trial.

details of the case. Other changes may take place that could work in the defendant's interest. If the process is delayed too long, the accused may never be tried or punished.

Before a trial, however, there must be an arraignment. In an arraignment, the accused is brought before a judge to answer the charges against him or her. The arraignment must be "without unnecessary delay." That rule was established in 1957 after a nineteen-year-old man named Mallory, of limited intelligence, was held overnight, questioned about a rape, and given two lie-detector tests. He was held in police custody from about 2:00 PM on April 7, 1954, until the next morning. During his questioning, Mallory confessed to several officers. Some attempt was made to arraign him that night, but he wasn't arraigned until the morning of April 8. During his lie-detector tests and his questioning, Mallory was not told that he had the rights to counsel, to remain silent, and to a preliminary examination (the investigation before a trial) in front of a judge.

Because of the delay before Mallory's arraignment, the Supreme Court decided, in *Mallory* v. *McNabb* (1957), to reverse both his conviction for rape and the death sentence. Mallory was released. Afterward, he committed a burglary and rape and was sentenced to twenty-two years in prison. He was released in a little over half that time. Then he robbed a couple and raped the woman and was fatally shot by police officers when he pulled a gun.

The *Mallory* case brought a great deal of unpleasant publicity to the Supreme Court. Congress accused the Court of letting a dangerous prisoner go free because of its "without unnecessary delay" decision.

The 1960s was a decade that brought great changes to the United States. Many communities that required segregation (the separation of people by race) were forced to desegregate, or put an end to segregation. There was great opposition to desegregation in many states. Those who wanted to desegregate public places often

An accused person being arraigned. In an arraignment, the accused is brought before a judge to answer the charges against him or her. In this case, the judge and others in the courtroom are well protected against any possible harm from the person being arraigned.

used peaceful means to achieve their aims. They marched, protested, and conducted sit-ins. In these sit-ins, people—often whites and blacks together—went to a public place and sat without moving until their demands were met. Many times the police were called to remove the protesters.

Out of this movement came the case that incorporated the right to a speedy trial. Peter Klopfer, a professor at Duke University in North Carolina, took part in a sit-in to desegregate a restaurant in 1964. He was tried for criminal trespass (illegally entering someone else's property). The jury was split, and a mistrial was declared. No second trial was scheduled. After a year, Professor Klopfer made an official demand that he either be tried right away or have the court dismiss the case.

Instead, the state's prosecutor made a legal motion that made Klopfer's indictment inactive but allowed the state to bring his case to trial sometime in the future. When Klopfer appealed, saying that his Sixth Amendment right to a speedy trial had been denied, the North Carolina Supreme Court declared that the right to a speedy trial didn't include "the right to compel [force] the state to prosecute him." Klopfer then made an appeal to the U.S. Supreme Court.

In *Klopfer* v. *North Carolina* (1967), the Court decided unanimously in favor of Klopfer. It said that he had "the right to a speedy trial which we hold is guaranteed to him [Klopfer] by the Sixth Amendment of the Constitution of the United States."

Sometimes there is an important reason for a state to delay a trial. This is what happened in *Barker* v. *Wingo* (1972), in Christian County, Kentucky. Willie Barker and Silas Manning were arrested for murdering an elderly couple in 1958. The state's case against Manning was stronger than its case against Barker, so Manning was tried first. The prosecutor hoped that Manning would be convicted and would then testify against Barker. The prosecutor had to convict Manning first so that he would not be forced to incriminate himself before a jury determined his guilt. Manning was tried three months after the murder took place, but the trial ended in a hung jury (a jury that cannot decide unanimously on a verdict). Several complications arose, and eventually Manning was tried five times before he was convicted of both murders. After each of Manning's trials in which no verdict was reached, the state asked for a continuance, or delay, of Barker's trial. Barker's lawyer didn't object to the first eleven continuances. The first objection was raised in 1962, when the prosecutor asked for the twelfth continuance. Meanwhile, except for the first ten months after his arrest, Barker remained out of jail and was able to live freely in his community.

Several more problems (such as the illness of the former sheriff who was scheduled to testify) came up, and more continuances were granted. Barker's trial finally began in September 1963, five years after he was first arrested. At the trial, Barker's lawyer moved to dismiss the charges because his client's right to a speedy trial had been violated. But the trial took place, Manning testified against Barker, and Barker was sentenced to life in prison.

After appeals to Kentucky's courts failed, Barker's case reached the Supreme Court. Although the Court had declared in a previous case that the right to a speedy trial is "as fundamental as any of the rights secured by the Sixth Amendment," it decided that Barker's right to a speedy trial had not been denied because there was a good reason for all the delays. Justice Byron White wrote the Court decision. He explained that there are no definite standards for deciding what a speedy trial is. He added that there is a cost to society as well as to the accused when there is no speedy trial. Barker, he said, was out on bail for four years. During that time, he had "an opportunity to commit other crimes." Delaying a trial, Justice White pointed out, is usually a defense tactic. Barker may not have objected to the first continuances because he hoped they would work in his favor. Barker "was gambling on Manning's acquittal."

In 1971, in a different case, the Supreme Court decided that an eighteen-month delay from arrest to trial didn't deprive a defendant of his right to a speedy trial. Over the years, the Court has also declared that in courts with an overload of cases, the accused isn't denied a speedy trial if his or her case isn't delayed longer than other trials. The Court added that the various levels of government should try to increase the number of judges and court workers so that cases can be brought to trial more quickly.

Many states and the federal government have "statutes of limitations." These are time periods after which certain crimes may not be prosecuted. In most places, there is no statute of limitations on murder cases.

In 1974, Congress passed the Federal Speedy Trial Act to try to deal with the issue of speedy trials in federal criminal cases. The law set time limits for various stages of criminal-justice proceedings. Under that law, both the prosecution and the defense could be punished for delaying the steps in a trial.

Two years after the Speedy Trial Act was passed, two men who weren't American citizens were released from custody because they hadn't been brought to trial within ninety days as the Speedy Trial Act required. The men fled across the Mexican border, and the U.S. Court of Appeals questioned the wisdom of Congress in creating the Speedy Trial Act. The court said that in addition to the scheduling problems the law had created, Congress had failed to add the judges and provide the money needed to make the time limits workable. In 1976, the Supreme Court agreed with the court of appeals, which said:

> We release a man alleged [declared without proof] to be the head of a foreign criminal organization dedicated to the smuggling of large quantities of illegal drugs, so that he may quickly cross the border and resume operating his business. We are also releasing his alleged right-hand man, as if to make certain that the enterprise continues to operate at top efficiency. But this result is the only one open to us under the plain terms of the statute [law]. It is discouraging that our highly refined and complex system of criminal justice is suddenly faced with implementing [carrying out] a statute that is so inartfully [poorly] drawn as this one. But this is the law and we are bound to give it effect.

In 1975, five men were arrested in Oregon for illegally transporting explosives and firearms. The prosecutor and the defense spent several years discussing which charges would be dismissed and which would not be. The failure to reach any agreement resulted in a long delay before the case went to trial. In 1983, the district court ruled that the defendants' right to a speedy trial had been violated and the charges were dismissed. But in 1986, the Supreme Court overturned the decisions of the lower courts. The Court ruled that there was "no showing of bad faith and dilatory [slowing] purpose on the government's part." The Court decision was by a 5 to 4 vote. The dissenting justices said that there was no excuse for the delay.

Public Trial

> Whatever other benefits the guarantee to an accused that his trial be conducted in public may confer upon our society, the guarantee has always been recognized as a safeguard against any attempt to employ our courts as instruments of persecution.

Justice Hugo Black made this comment in his majority opinion concerning a very strange case about the right to a public trial. *In re Oliver* (1948) involved the right to a jury trial for a man named William Oliver, who had been jailed by a Michigan "one-man grand jury."

Photographers and reporters have become an important part of the publicity that surrounds some trials. In dictatorships, on the other hand, trials are often conducted in secret.

The Fifth Amendment provides for a grand jury in cases involving serious crimes. Most states have grand juries that investigate to see whether a crime has been committed. If necessary, the grand jury presents indictments (formal accusations) against the person or persons who may be put on trial. Most grand juries have from twelve to twenty-three members. Their job is to see whether there is enough evidence to bring charges. Michigan had a different system that allowed a single judge to sit as a "grand jury" and determine whether there was enough evidence to present charges.

William Oliver received a subpoena to appear before the judge who was conducting a one-man grand jury investigation into possible gambling and corruption. Oliver appeared before the judge without counsel and gave his testimony. In the middle of the questioning, the judge said Oliver's story did not "jell." The judge charged him with contempt of court (showing disrespect for the court), a charge that doesn't require a jury trial. He sentenced Oliver to sixty days in jail.

The judge based his opinion on testimony that another witness had given in secret. Oliver didn't even know about that witness's testimony. He certainly didn't have a chance to challenge it or prepare a defense. In effect, William Oliver had been tried in a secret trial and had been found guilty of a crime without knowing the charges. Oliver had no chance to confront witnesses or to challenge their testimony. He had no lawyer or time to prepare a defense and no jury. The "trial" (or nontrial) violated almost all of the rights a person would have under the Sixth Amendment.

The Supreme Court ruled that the Sixth Amendment right to a public trial applies in a state criminal trial. It therefore reversed the charges against Oliver. The Court said:

> It is "the law of the land" that no man's life, liberty or property be forfeited as a punishment until there has been a charge fairly made and fairly tried in a public tribunal. . . . The petitioner [Oliver] was convicted without that kind of trial.

In re Oliver (1948) made the right to a public trial binding upon the states. Oliver had been sentenced on the basis of a contempt of court charge, a charge upon which many individuals have been sentenced without a public trial. In 1958, Justice Hugo Black warned of the possible danger in a judge's power to punish people for criminal contempt. He said it was "nearest akin to despotic power of any power existing under our form of government... usurping [seizing] our regular constitutional methods of trying those charged with offenses against society."

Yet at times it is necessary for a judge to charge someone with contempt of court. Some defendants scream and get violent in the courtroom. So do some people attending the trial. A judge may have the courtroom cleared so that people watching the trial don't interfere with the legal process. Usually, however, the defendant has a right to be present. How does a judge deal with an unruly defendant who is interfering with the trial?

In 1970, the Supreme Court gave its opinion on how a judge should deal with contempt of court when a defendant misbehaves in the courtroom. The Court was unanimous in declaring that violation of "elementary standards of proper conduct should not and cannot be tolerated." The Court suggested three ways in which a judge could deal with "an obstreperous [noisy and unruly] defendant": (1) bind and gag him, (2) cite him for contempt, and (3) take him out of the courtroom until he can behave properly.

Is a defendant required to have a public trial, or can he or she waive (give up) that right? Several times, the Supreme Court has decided that a defendant may waive the right to a public trial, but that the prosecutor may not take that right from someone who wants a public trial. Many defendants choose to avoid a public trial when they accept a plea bargain. A plea bargain is an agreement between the accused and the prosecutor. The accused usually agrees to plead guilty to a lesser charge than the one that could be made at the trial. In exchange, the prosecutor agrees to a sentence that is less severe than the one the accused could receive if he or she were found guilty by a jury. There is no public trial.

For many years, plea bargains were done behind the scenes but not admitted in public. In 1971, the Supreme Court officially admitted that plea bargains existed and were legal. The Court did so when it ruled on the case of *Santobello* v. *New York.* Santobello, the defendant, had made an agreement for a plea bargain. But when he reached the courtroom, he faced a different prosecutor and a different judge from those who knew of his agreement. There was no record of the plea bargain. The Court said plea bargains are acceptable, but a record must be kept of the agreement and the prosecutor has to keep his side of the bargain.

In 1978, the Supreme Court considered *Bordenkircher* v. *Hayes.* This case involved a prosecutor who threatened to inflict a heavier punishment if Paul Lewis Hayes, the accused, refused to accept a plea bargain. The Court ruled that it is unconstitutional for a prosecutor to threaten a life sentence "if the only objective . . . is to discourage the assertion of constitutional rights." Hayes had the right to a public trial, and the prosecutor shouldn't have threatened a life sentence just to force him to give up this right.

Plea bargains save the state a great deal of time and money, but there are drawbacks to the system. Both guilty and innocent people have accepted plea bargains to avoid the possibility of receiving a more severe sentence from a jury. And both guilty and innocent people have refused plea bargains because they hoped a jury would acquit them.

When the Court declared that plea bargains are not unconstitutional, it said:

> This mode [method] of conviction is no more foolproof than full trials to the court or to the jury. Accordingly, we take great precautions against unsound results, and we should continue to do so, whether conviction is by plea or by trial.

If the accused person is entitled to a public trial, does that give newspapers and other media the "right to know"? Does the public have a "right to know" about trials? Newspapers tend to cover certain kinds of trials and ignore others. Radio and television reporters want to broadcast the proceedings in some courtrooms. Often the reporters aren't impartial, and either the defendant's side or the prosecutor's side is reported more favorably. Is the right of the press to report a trial as it chooses guaranteed by the First and Sixth Amendments? These questions have come before the Supreme Court many times.

Newspaper reporters are allowed into courtrooms—sometimes as part of the general public, sometimes in special press sections. In 1965, the Supreme Court ruled that radio and television reporters have the same rights that newspaper reporters have, but they don't have a constitutional right to bring in microphones or cameras:

> The press reporter is not permitted to bring his typewriter or printing press. When the advances in these arts permit reporting by printing press or by television without their present hazards to a fair trial we will have another case.

In several other cases, the Court ruled that the Sixth Amendment right to a public trial was for the benefit of the defendant, not for the public. The defendant's right to a fair trial was more important than the public's "right to know," a right that the Court doesn't recognize. In 1979, Justice Potter Stewart wrote:

> [R]ecognition of an independent public interest in the enforcement of Sixth Amendment guarantees is a far cry . . . from the creation of a constitutional right on the part of the public.

One very sensational case raised the issue of how a trial that is too public could make it impossible to maintain an impartial, or fair, jury. The next chapter tells that story.

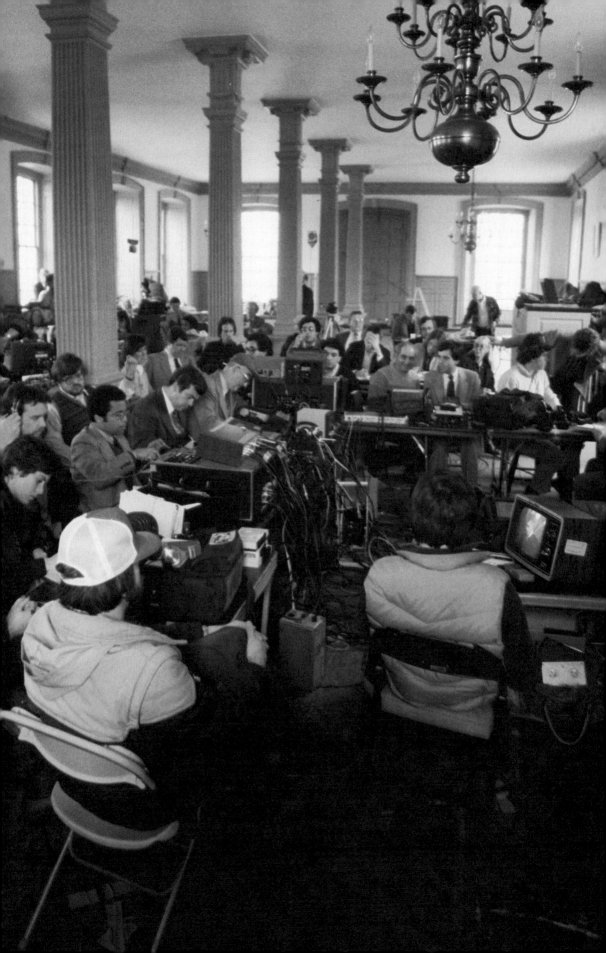

The Right to an Impartial Jury and a Fair Trial

"The guarantees of jury trial in the Federal and State Constitutions reflect a profound [deeply felt] judgment about the way in which law should be enforced and justice administered."

JUSTICE BYRON R. WHITE, in *Duncan* v. *Louisiana* (1968)

The trial of Dr. Samuel Sheppard, who was accused of murdering his wife, had been fully covered in the media (newspapers, radio, and television) both before the trial and while it was taking place in a suburb of Cleveland, Ohio, in 1954.

Mrs. Sheppard was murdered in an upstairs bedroom while Dr. Sheppard slept downstairs. He heard nobody in the house and wandered around dazed for a while. Within a few days, Mrs. Sheppard's relatives were certain that Dr. Sheppard had committed the murder, but he denied it. Before the trial began, newspapers printed pictures of Mrs. Sheppard. They told what a wonderful person she was and demanded that her murderer be punished. They suggested that Dr. Sheppard would try to get away with the murder because he had many important friends. Even before the trial began, the Cleveland newspapers had decided that Dr. Sheppard was guilty and called for his punishment.

Many prospective jurors (people who could be called to serve on juries) had read news stories about the doctor. Newspapers printed

---

Reporters at a murder trial watch the proceedings and file their reports to their TV, radio, or press offices. They must take care not to interfere unfairly with the jury's deliberations or with the testimony of witnesses.

the names, addresses, and telephone numbers of all prospective jurors and of those who were actually chosen for the doctor's jury. Jury members received many letters and phone calls from strangers about the upcoming trial. Because of all the publicity and jury involvement, the defense asked for the trial to be moved to another county.

It was a very public trial, but many details that were covered in the media during the trial were never presented at the trial. The prosecutor leaked information to reporters. Most of this so-called evidence wasn't presented at the trial, and much of it wouldn't have been allowed by a judge. But members of the jury could and did read the stories.

Most of the seats in the courtroom were reserved for members of the media. These seats included extra seats placed directly behind the defendant and his lawyer, making it impossible for them to carry on private discussions. The judge and city officials allowed reporters to talk to witnesses and jurors and to have access to trial exhibits (items used for evidence in the trial).

Radio and television news people reported rumors and inaccurate information. During the trial, the defendant's lawyer objected to the jury's exposure to all the news stories about details that weren't part of the trial. The judge said he was unable to stop it. Yet he did ask Dr. Sheppard's brother to stop "trying the case in the newspapers" and threatened to remove him from the courtroom.

After Dr. Sheppard was found guilty of second-degree murder, he began a series of appeals based on the claim that he had been denied an impartial jury. The Supreme Court agreed with him. It referred to the "carnival atmosphere" at the trial. In *Sheppard* v. *Maxwell* (1966), the Court said that Sheppard had to be released unless the state wanted to try him again within a reasonable amount of time. It stated:

Had the judge, the other officers of the court, and the police placed the interest of justice first, the news media would have soon learned to be content with the task of reporting the case as it unfolded in the

During the 1954 murder trial of Dr. Sam Sheppard, reporters were eager to interview jurors and report all sorts of rumors. The Supreme Court later commented on the "carnival atmosphere" of the trial.

courtroom. . . . Due process requires that the accused receive a fair trial by an impartial jury free from outside influences.

The Court pointed out that the trial judge could have "at least warned the newspapers to check the accuracy of their accounts." The judge could have limited the number of the reporters in the courtroom. In addition, he could have refused to allow statements to the media or public by lawyers, witnesses, court officials, and others connected with the trial.

The Sixth Amendment right to a fair trial clashed again with the First Amendment right to a free press in a case involving a television news station and a former ruler of another country. In 1990, Cable News Network (CNN) announced it would broadcast

People followed the Sheppard murder trial very closely. Information not presented at the trial was at times leaked to the press and read by a curious public. People were eager to learn all they could about the Sheppards.

tapes of General Manuel Noriega talking to his lawyers. Noriega, the former dictator of Panama, was accused of shipping illegal drugs into the United States and was to stand trial in Florida.

Both the U.S. government and Noriega's lawyers tried to prevent CNN from broadcasting the tapes. Many people would hear or read about the tapes. Even if the taped conversation wasn't permitted in court, jurors could already have formed an opinion about Noriega based on the tapes. The government feared that the broadcast would make a fair trial impossible and thus make it impossible to convict Noriega.

CNN did play part of the tapes. But a federal court ordered CNN to stop. The Supreme Court approved of a temporary stop to the public playing of the tapes. That would allow the lower federal court judge a few days to decide whether the public playing of the tapes would affect a fair trial. Within a few days the Federal court judge said that CNN could play the tapes.

Incorporation of the Right to an Impartial Trial

In 1966, the right to an impartial trial was incorporated in a different case—one involving a sequestered jury. Juries are often sequestered. This means that the members of the jury are kept separated from the public. Sequestering a jury prevents jurors from hearing rumors and opinions that are not part of the trial. But in Lee Parker's trial, the bailiff (a court official whose name was Gladden), remarked to the sequestered jury, "Oh, that wicked fellow, he is guilty." In *Parker* v. *Gladden* (1966), the Supreme Court decided that Parker had been denied his Sixth Amendment right to an impartial trial because of the bailiff's remark.

A jury may fail to be impartial because of interference from outside sources, but it may also be unfair because of the way it is organized. Although both Article III of the Constitution and the Sixth Amendment require a fair jury trial, neither says what a jury is or who should serve on it.

In England it was traditional to have juries of twelve free men. (Women couldn't serve.) The United States followed the English custom, except that by 1930, some women did serve on juries if they volunteered to do so. When the question of what made up a legal jury arose in 1930, Justice George Sutherland declared that a trial by jury should follow English and American common law:

(1) that the jury should consist of twelve men, neither more nor less;
(2) that the trial should be in the presence and under the superinten-

dence of a judge having power to instruct them as to the law and advise them in respect to facts; and (3) that the verdict should be unanimous.

Except for the fact that women are now called for jury duty in the same way that men are called, these rules remain for trials in *federal* courts. The jury has to have twelve members. The verdict has to be unanimous. If even one of the twelve jurors disagrees with the majority, there can be no verdict.

Before long, questions about state trials arose. Could a defendant waive the right to a jury trial? Could a jury have eight or six jurors instead of twelve? Must a verdict be unanimous? Each of these questions reached the Supreme Court.

During the 1970s, the Supreme Court decided that some federal rules need not apply to state juries. The Court declared that state juries may have only six members, but not fewer than six. State-court jury verdicts do not have to be unanimous for twelve-member juries. But unanimous decisions are required for six-member juries. One justice commented that he wasn't sure that he would willingly accept a split decision of 7 to 5 from a twelve-member jury, but the Supreme Court was not faced with an actual case where that occurred.

The right to have a jury trial became an issue in several important cases. Special problems arise during wartime, and the Court has to balance the rights of the accused against military needs.

Toward the end of the Civil War, a Southern sympathizer (someone who lived in the North but sympathized with the cause of the South) named Lambdin P. Milligan was arrested on the orders of the Union general in charge of the Indiana military district. Milligan, a civilian (a person who is not in the armed forces), had been encouraging insurrection (rebellion) against the Union. He was tried in a military court and sentenced to be hanged. Milligan appealed the sentence, claiming that he had a right to a trial by a jury.

The Supreme Court made its decision in 1866, after the Civil War had ended. It agreed with Milligan, although the justices had different reasons for their decision. The majority opinion of the Court noted that Milligan wasn't a citizen of one of the Confederate states. He wasn't a prisoner of war. He was never in military service, and he had lived in Indiana for twenty years. Indiana wasn't a war zone, which would have made military law appropriate. There was no reason that Milligan couldn't have been tried in an Indiana court and received a fair verdict and punishment.

The Court expressed concern that the presidency could at some time become occupied by "[w]icked men, ambitious of power, with hatred for liberty and contempt of law," and the Framers of the Constitution and the Bill of Rights had to establish safeguards of civil liberties against such possibilities. Jury trials were part of that safeguard.

Throughout much of the country's history, members of certain groups were not called up for jury service. If they were called, they weren't permitted to serve. For many years, African Americans weren't selected for juries, especially in Southern states. In a series of cases, black defendants who were tried by all-white juries appealed to the Supreme Court. They claimed that they had been denied the right to an impartial jury—in this case, one that included people of their own race. Time after time, the Court declared juries that excluded blacks, or kept them off, to be unconstitutional. But they continued to exist.

As early as 1880, in *Strauder* v. *West Virginia*, the Supreme Court began hearing cases regarding juries that excluded African Americans. In that year, the Court agreed that a Virginia county court judge should not have eliminated African Americans from his jury lists. But the Court also decided that African Americans weren't specifically entitled to have African-American jurors decide their cases.

"The Southern states adjusted themselves to these two judicial rules by the simple process of avoiding any open discrimination against blacks in the calling of grand or petit juries," noted Robert Cushman, an authority on the Bill of Rights, "and yet no names of blacks found their way on to the jury lists and no black person was ever called for jury service."

African Americans were still being excluded from most juries when the "Scottsboro boys" were tried for rape in Alabama in 1931. They won their first Supreme Court case, *Powell* v. *Alabama* (1932), because they had no real counsel at the trial. The *Powell* case incorporated the right to counsel in capital cases. But the young men weren't set free. They were tried again, this time in Decatur, Alabama.

The Decatur trials began on March 27, 1933. This time the defendants were represented by Samuel S. Liebowitz, a well-known lawyer from New York. He started out by saying that the grand jury that indicted the defendants was illegal because only whites had served on it. First, he proved that, in both Scottsboro and Decatur, African Americans weren't called for jury duty. When an official responsible for jury lists in the Decatur area was called, Liebowitz asked if all the names in the jury list were white. The answer was, "I don't know." Because several white officials suggested that African Americans weren't capable of being jurors, ten well-educated African Americans of the district testified that they had never been called for jury duty.

Although the judge wouldn't stop the trial, he did agree that there seemed to be a good case for showing that African Americans had been excluded from juries.

At the trial, most of the witnesses were the same people who had testified in Scottsboro in 1931. The main witness was one of the women who claimed to have been raped. Her story contradicted itself and changed at each trial. The prosecutor and his assistant made remarks that showed they were prejudiced against both African Americans and the Jewish lawyer. But their prejudices seemed to agree with those of the jurors, and the boys were convicted once again. Judge James Edwin Horton, Jr., however, indicated that he didn't believe that the boys were guilty or that a crime had even taken place. When the verdicts were appealed, Horton agreed that new trials should be held.

A different judge heard the new trials. Once again, the defendants were found guilty. The cases were appealed to the Supreme Court. The appeal was based on the fact that the defendants had been tried by an all-white jury from which African Americans had been excluded. In this 1935 case, *Norris* v. *Alabama* (the *Second Scottsboro* case), the Supreme Court agreed with Clarence Norris that his Sixth Amendment rights, guaranteed by the Fourteenth Amendment, had been violated. But the Supreme Court's decisions didn't lead to immediate freedom for any of the young men. The last of the "Scottsboro boys," Andrew Wright, wasn't set free until 1950.

In 1942, the Supreme Court gave additional support to people who believed they hadn't been tried by an impartial jury. The Court said that when no African Americans had served on juries in a district for sixteen years, the defendant didn't have to prove that juries were deliberately segregated. Instead, the state had to prove that it didn't deliberately eliminate African Americans. As states found new ways to keep African Americans off juries, the Court kept overturning the convictions of people who had been convicted by segregated juries.

This series of cases reveals what the Supreme Court may or may not do in deciding cases. It can overturn a conviction if it was based on an unconstitutional practice. Although the Court can send cases back to lower courts with orders to make changes, people who don't want to change may try new ways to get around the law. Most levels of government go along with constitutional procedures because they don't want to see convictions overturned. But the Court cannot interfere before a trial begins or during the trial.

Mexican Americans proved that people with Hispanic last names had been kept off a county's jury lists for twenty-five years.

In *Hernandez* v. *Texas* (1954), the Supreme Court overturned the conviction of a Mexican American who had been tried by a jury in that county.

People don't have to belong to the group that is excluded in order to appeal a case in which some group has been excluded. In 1972, the Court heard a case from a white man who claimed that he didn't have an impartial jury because African Americans had been excluded. Six members of the Supreme Court agreed with him. They said that racial discrimination in choosing jurors does not make for an impartial jury.

If juries from which African Americans or Hispanic Americans had been excluded weren't impartial, what about juries with no women? During most of the history of the jury system, women weren't allowed to serve on juries. After 1920, when women won the right to vote in national elections, some states called them for jury duty. During the 1960s, seventeen states had systems in which women could volunteer to serve on juries, but they weren't required to do so.

Gwendolyn Hoyt claimed that she hadn't received a fair trial because Florida didn't require women to serve on juries, and no women were called for her jury. The Supreme Court didn't agree. In *Hoyt* v. *Florida* (1961), it decided unanimously that the Florida law didn't exclude women and therefore wasn't illegal.

By 1975, times had changed. Many women now worked outside their homes and were demanding equal rights. Laws that excused them from jury duty just because they were women didn't make sense. A man named Taylor was tried in Louisiana, and he appealed the decision because women weren't required to serve on his jury. In *Taylor* v. *Louisiana* (1975), the Supreme Court changed its mind about the *Hoyt* decision. The Court declared that state laws that did not require women to be called for jury duty violated the Sixth Amendment guarantee of a fair, impartial jury. A jury that excluded more than half the population couldn't really represent the community.

The Supreme Court's opinion on impartial juries seems to be clear. Court officers and the media may not interfere with the jury process. Juries that exclude certain groups in a community are unconstitutional, but no defendant has the specific right to have jurors of his or her own race, ethnic or religious group, or gender on a particular jury.

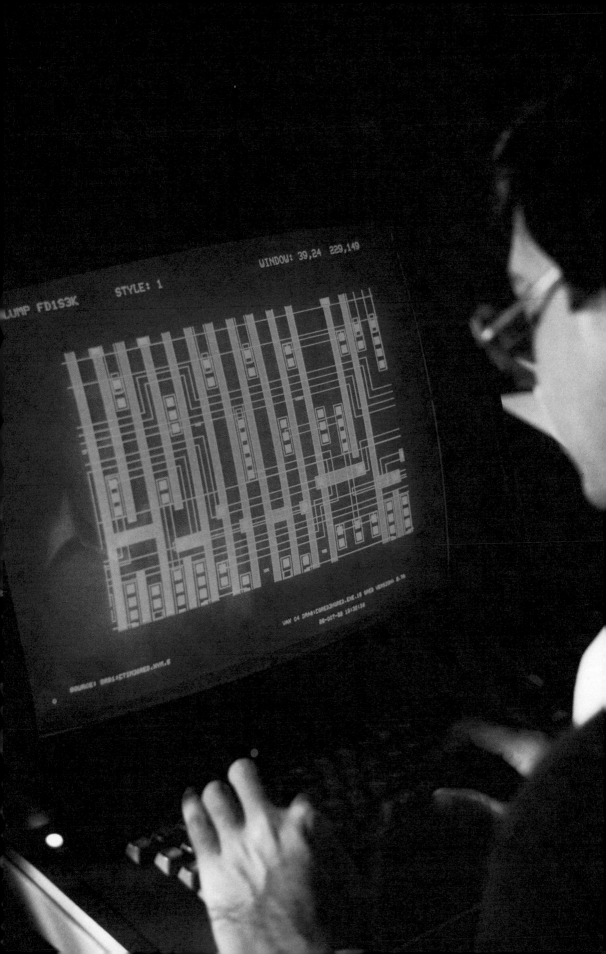

CHAPTER 6

The Right to Be Tried in the District and Be Informed of the Charges

"In all criminal prosecutions, the accused shall enjoy the right to . . . be informed of the cause and nature of the accusation. . . ."

"The trial of all crimes . . . shall be by an impartial jury of freeholders of the vicinage, with the requisite [requirement] of unanimity for conviction. . . ."

JAMES MADISON, First Draft of Proposed Amendment

In the very first draft of the amendments that James Madison suggested for the Constitution, he included the ideas that eventually became part of the Sixth Amendment. The wording "cause and nature of his accusation" came directly from the Virginia Declaration of Rights (1776).

The term *vicinage*, meaning neighborhood, remained in the second and third drafts of Madison's proposed amendments. In the final version, however, it was changed to "State and district wherein the crime shall have been committed." This wording was much clearer.

State and District

The defense counsel in the *Sheppard* case asked for a change of venue (a move of the trial to another district). That is the defendant's right. As with the right to a public trial, it is the defendant who has the right to be tried in the state and district in which the crime took place. The state may not change the venue on its own.

Crimes are supposed to be tried in the state and district where they occurred. Inventions such as radios, computers, and other means of communication, as well as large corporations with branches all over the world, have made it more difficult to determine just *where* a crime occurred.

The accused, however, may ask to have the trial moved to a different place if there is strong evidence that a fair trial or an impartial jury would be difficult or impossible to get in the "State and district wherein the crime shall have been committed."

The privilege of moving a trial is often requested when a crime has received a great deal of publicity before the trial. It may also be requested when there is reason to believe that the accused can't get a fair trial in the neighborhood in which the crime took place. For example, after the first Scottsboro trials, the venue was moved to Decatur, Alabama. Many defendants who ask for a change of venue are not granted their request because the judge does not agree that there is enough reason to move the trial to another district.

Moving a trial to another place involves many practical problems. When a trial is moved, all the witnesses for both the prosecution and the defense must be able to appear at the new location. All the pieces of evidence must also be moved. Moving a trial involves additional expenses and many complications. Those are good reasons that most judges are cautious about granting requests for a change of venue. The right to a change of venue applies to any crimes that are tried by a judge. This includes misdemeanors as well as felonies. A felony is any serious crime punishable by death or by a prison term of more than a year. A misdemeanor is any crime less serious than a felony.

The Federal Rules of Criminal Procedure, established in 1947 for federal trials, said that a defendant must be granted a change of venue if there is "so great a prejudice against the defendant that he [or she] cannot obtain a fair and impartial trial" at any court in the district. Each state has its own standard for changing venue, but most standards are very strict.

Some crimes are not limited to one state or one district. People living in two different places may get together to plot to commit a crime in a third place. Since many crimes today can be committed by mail, telephone, or computer, a government—state or federal— has to decide where such crimes will be tried. Sometimes one "party" in a criminal trial is a large corporation that operates in many districts and states.

At one time, the federal government often moved a defendant to a far-off place for trial if there was any link between the far-off place and the crime. But Congress eventually set up rules for deciding where a federal crime will be tried or whether a change of venue should be granted or refused.

In a 1964 case involving a large corporation, the Supreme Court listed several considerations for a judge who has to decide whether to grant a change of venue:

1. location of corporate defendant;
2. location of possible witnesses;
3. location of events likely to be in issue;
4. location of documents and records likely to be involved;
5. disruption of defendant's business unless the case is transferred;
6. expense to the parties;
7. location of counsel;
8. relative accessibility of place of trial;
9. docket [list of cases to be tried] condition of each district or division involved; and
10. any other special elements which might affect the transfer

When a federal law has been violated, but not in any particular state or district, Congress decides where the trial will be held. An example of a federal crime of this kind might be a theft on an overseas U.S. military base by a military dependent. The dependent (the husband, wife, or child of someone in the armed forces) may be sent back to the United States for trial because neither the laws of the country in which he or she is stationed nor U.S. military laws would be in effect. But U.S. laws would govern the crime.

The civil rights movement of the 1960s set out to put an end to segregation. Civil rights workers from many states went to the

South to help desegregate public places and to help African Americans register to vote. Many civil rights workers and many African Americans were arrested by the police in the South. The federal government wanted to move some cases out of the local courts because federal lawyers believed that juries in the state and district would be biased against civil rights workers. The federal government would have preferred to try the cases in federal courts, but in most cases it didn't have the right to do so.

A group of civil rights workers who were arrested in Mississippi in 1964 on violations of local laws asked to have their cases tried in the federal court instead of in a local court. In 1966, the Supreme Court decided against the civil rights workers in this and other, similar cases.

Unlike other Sixth Amendment provisions, the "state and district" clause did not have to be incorporated because it specifically applies to the state and the district.

The Nature and Cause of the Accusation

There are many countries in the world today in which people are arrested and imprisoned without ever being told why. If a person doesn't know what crime he or she is supposed to have committed, there is no way of proving innocence. Dictatorships thrive on the power to arrest and imprison people without having to provide a reason.

In the United States, charges made against a person must be clear. They have to provide a standard against which guilt or innocence can be measured. In 1939, the Court declared, in *Lanzetta* v. *New Jersey*, that a person can't be convicted for being a "gangster" without a clear definition of the term *gangster* and charges of specific violations of laws.

Above all, a person shouldn't be convicted without proof that a crime has actually been committed. Yet that's exactly what happened in Louisville, Kentucky, when a man named Thompson was convicted of "loitering and disorderly conduct."

At about 6:20 PM on a Saturday evening in January 1959, Thompson went into the Liberty End Cafe. When two policemen entered the café for a routine check about a half hour later, they saw Thompson "out there on the floor dancing by himself." They asked the manager how long Thompson had been in the café and whether he had bought anything. At that time, the manager didn't remember whether Thompson had bought food or drink. Then the policemen asked Thompson what he was doing in the café. He answered that he was waiting for a bus. The officers arrested Thompson and took him outside. He argued with them, and they charged him with disorderly conduct.

Thompson had been arrested fifty-four times before. He argued that to convict him of this crime based on his previous record would deny him his right to due process under the law. He asked that the charges be dismissed, saying that there was no evidence to find him guilty. His request was denied.

Thompson's own testimony said that he bought food and beer in the café and then waited for a bus to return home. He had money on him, and a bus was scheduled to stop near the café at 7:30 PM. He wasn't a "vagrant" (unemployed homeless wanderer) because he had regular work and a place in which to live. The manager of the café testified that Thompson often came to the café and had never been told that he wasn't welcome there. At the trial, the manager added that he had seen Thompson "standing there in the middle of the floor and patting his foot" and he (the manager) didn't find anything wrong with that behavior. Nevertheless, the court found Thompson guilty and fined him $10 on each of the two charges.

Thompson appealed, and the Supreme Court accepted his case. The Court noted that "although the fines here are small, the due process questions presented here are substantial. . . ." The Court decided that there was no evidence to support the charges. Thompson wasn't loitering because according to Louisville law, loitering means that a person has "no visible means of support" or "cannot give a satisfactory account of himself." He had money on him, and he was able to give an account of himself. Louisville had no law against dancing, shuffling, or patting the feet, so Thompson's behavior in the café wasn't illegal. The Court summed up its opinion:

> Just as "Conviction upon a charge not made would be sheer denial of due process," so is it a violation of due process to convict and punish a man without evidence of his guilt.

The case of *Thompson* v. *Louisville* (1960) dealt with an accusation of a very small crime and an equally small punishment. Yet the principle behind the appeal and the Court's decision was anything but small. No one can be convicted and punished without evidence of guilt. Thompson wasn't told the "nature and cause of the accusation," so he couldn't prove that he wasn't guilty. He had been convicted of a crime without any evidence that a crime had actually been committed. By accepting and deciding such cases as *Thompson*, the Supreme Court helps keep the other courts of the land from overstepping their authority.

The Supreme Court has overturned state and local laws that it considered to be too vague to be useful. In 1972, in *Papachristou et al.* v. *City of Jacksonville*, the Court looked at the "vagrancy laws" of Jacksonville, Florida. One of these laws stated:

> Rogues and vagabonds [wanderers], or dissolute [wicked] persons who go about begging, common gamblers, persons who use juggling or unlawful games or plays, common drunkards, common night walkers, thieves, pilferers [petty thieves] or pickpockets, traders in stolen property, lewd, wanton and lascivious [lustful] persons, keepers of gambling places, common railers [angry complainers] and brawlers, persons wandering or strolling around from place to place without any lawful purpose or object, habitual loafers, disorderly persons, persons neglecting all lawful business and habitually spending their time by frequenting houses of ill fame, gaming houses, or places where alcoholic beverages are sold or served, persons able to work but habitually living upon the earnings of their wives or minor children shall be deemed vagrants and upon conviction in the Municipal Court shall be punished as provided for Class D offenses.

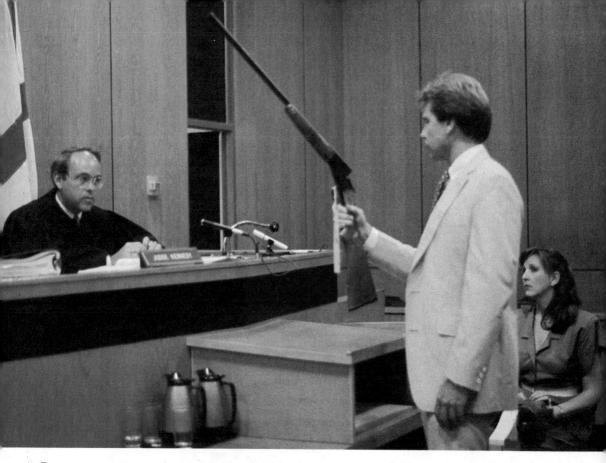

Prosecutors must not conceal evidence they know might help an accused person prove his or her innocence.

The Court overruled this law, and Justice William O. Douglas wrote:

> A presumption that people who might walk or loaf or loiter or stroll or frequent houses where liquor is sold, or who are supported by their wives or who look suspicious to the police are to become future criminals is too precarious [risky] for a rule of law.

In 1985, the Supreme Court declared that the prosecutor must let the accused know about any evidence that might help this person prove his or her innocence.

In all criminal cases, the prosecutor has the burden of proof. This means that the prosecutor must prove that a defendant committed the crime. Since 1985, the prosecutor—not the defendant—must also prove criminal intent (the intention to commit a crime).

The Right to Confront and Subpoena Witnesses

"We hold today that the Sixth Amendment's right of an accused to confront the witnesses against him is likewise a fundamental right and is made obligatory on the States by the Fourteenth Amendment."

JUSTICE HUGO L. BLACK, in *Pointer* v. *Texas* (1965)

People who want to end neighborhood criminal activity, such as drug dealing, often suggest that they should be able to call the police anonymously (without giving their names) to report crimes. Many people want to remain anonymous because they are afraid that the criminals they report will harm them or their families.

A police officer isn't allowed to arrest anybody based on anonymous information. Sometimes police officers use anonymous information as a lead to do their own investigating. But in order for a case to be brought to trial, there must be witnesses and/or evidence. It isn't enough to tell a judge, "Everybody in the neighborhood knows that gang is dealing drugs." Somebody—an ordinary citizen or a police officer—has to confront, or face, a defendant at the trial.

While law-abiding people may wish that criminals could be sent to jail on anonymous evidence, those who have been wrongly

Associate Justice Sandra Day O'Connor was appointed to the Supreme Court in 1981. O'Connor wrote the 1990 majority opinion in a case concerning whether children who may have been victims of child abuse had to face the adults they had accused. The Court decided that a defendant's lawyer could question the very young accuser, but on closed-circuit television.

accused of crimes are glad to know that Americans have the right to confront the witnesses against them and to subpoena their own witnesses. The same rights that protect criminals also protect innocent people.

Confronting the Witnesses

A defendant has the right to confront witnesses and to try to prove that their testimony is untrue or unreliable. What happens when the witnesses are FBI agents? Must they reveal the sources of their information? That question arose during the trial of Clinton Jencks, a union leader with Communist beliefs who was suspected of perjury (giving false information while testifying under oath). Jencks wasn't given the opportunity to disprove the testimony of FBI agents who had testified at his trial because he couldn't question the sources of their information. The information from the sources was given only through the FBI agents.

Jencks was found guilty. He appealed his conviction, saying that he didn't have an opportunity to confront the witnesses against him. In *Jencks* v. *United States* (1957), the Supreme Court agreed and Jencks's conviction was overturned. In its decision, the Court quoted an earlier ruling that said "the interest of the United States in a criminal prosecution . . . is not that it shall win a case, but that justice shall be done."

Eight years later, the right to confront a witness was fully incorporated when the Supreme Court heard the case of *Pointer* v. *Texas* (1965). Granville Pointer and Earl Dillard had been charged with robbing a man named Kenneth Phillips. Phillips testified at the preliminary hearing, the investigation before a trial. At the hearing, Phillips identified Pointer, who was present but had no lawyer there.

During a trial, each side has the right to cross-examine witnesses from the other side. This means that the other side can ask questions about the witness's testimony. Cross-examination may help show whether the testimony is reliable or accurate.

At the preliminary hearing, nobody cross-examined Phillips on Pointer's behalf. But a record of Phillips's testimony was kept. By the time of Pointer's trial, Phillips had moved from Texas to California and didn't intend to return to Texas. The prosecutor used Phillips's testimony from the preliminary hearing at Pointer's trial. Pointer's lawyer objected to allowing the jury to hear the testimony Phillips had given unless Phillips was present. The lawyer claimed that his client didn't have a chance to cross-examine Phillips because Phillips wasn't present at the trial. The trial judge over-ruled the objections. He said that Pointer could have cross-examined Phillips at the preliminary hearing. Phillips's testimony at the preliminary hearing was permitted, and Pointer was found guilty.

The Supreme Court unanimously reversed Pointer's conviction in *Pointer* v. *Texas* (1965). Justice Hugo Black wrote the Court's opinion:

> We hold today that the Sixth Amendment's right of an accused to confront the witnesses against him is likewise a fundamental right and is made obligatory on the States by the Fourteenth Amendment.

From 1965 on, defendants in state courts had the same right as defendants in federal courts: the right to confront witnesses against them. The *Pointer* decision reversed a 1904 ruling that said the right to confront a witness was not guaranteed in state trials.

Pointer won his case in the Supreme Court, but he was tried again in Texas. This time Phillips appeared at his trial, and Pointer was found guilty once again.

The Supreme Court's rulings don't guarantee that people who have been convicted of crimes will go free if their convictions are found to be unconstitutional. The only thing the Court reversals accomplish is seeing to it that people who are convicted or freed are treated in keeping with the Constitution. Pointer wasn't the first person to win a Supreme Court case and lose in a retrial.

The *Pointer* case incorporated the right to confront unfriendly witnesses. But what about witnesses whose testimony could be helpful if the accused could confront them or harmful if the accused could not confront them? A co-defendant (another defendant in the same trial) in a trial made a confession but did not take the stand. That meant that the defendant on trial had no opportunity to cross-examine the co-defendant. In *Bruton* v. *United States* (1968), the Court declared that "the admission of a confession of a co-defendant who did not take the stand deprived the defendant of his rights under the Sixth Amendment Confrontation Clause."

The Court allows some exceptions to this rule. One exception arises if a witness has given testimony and has been cross-examined by the defendant at a previous proceeding but is not available at the time of the trial. But the witness has to be truly unavailable for the trial.

A defendant has the right to be in the courtroom during the trial. Can a trial continue if a defendant isn't in the courtroom? Does the defendant's absence violate his or her right to face the accuser? In 1970, the Court ruled that a defendant may be removed from a courtroom if his or her behavior makes it impossible to conduct the trial (for example, if a defendant won't stop shouting or interrupting the questioning). The trial can continue as long as the defendant's lawyer is present. This doesn't deny the defendant's right to confront a witness.

Confrontation of witnesses has taken a new turn in the electronic age. May videotaped or televised testimony be produced at a trial if the witness is not present?

This question has become especially important when the witnesses are very young children who are testifying in cases of abuse. Abused children are usually terrified of the adults who have harmed them. These children are frightened of telling about their experiences when the accused abuser is in the same room with them.

Courts have been looking for ways to allow children to testify about their experiences without having to testify in the presence of the defendant. One solution to this problem was to allow children to use closed-circuit television to give their testimony. But many states were confused about whether such testimony was permitted by the Constitution.

In 1990, the Supreme Court considered two cases involving confrontation of witnesses and children. It gave a 5 to 4 decision in each. In *Maryland* v. *Craig* (1990), the Court ruled that children who are believed to be victims of child abuse may give their testimony on closed-circuit television and that they do not have to be confronted by the people they have accused. Justice Sandra Day O'Connor wrote the decision. In it she said that the right to a face-to-face confrontation was important, but it was not an "indispensable [absolutely necessary] element" of the Sixth Amendment guarantee of confrontation. She added:

[A] state's interest in the physical and psychological well-being of child abuse victims may be sufficiently important to outweigh, at least in some cases, a defendant's right to face his or her accusers in court.

When a child is allowed to give testimony on closed-circuit television, the defendant's lawyer still has the right to question the child.

Justice Antonin Scalia wrote a sharp dissent to the *Maryland* v. *Craig* (1990) decision. He said, "Seldom has this Court failed so conspicuously [obviously] to sustain a categorical guarantee of the Constitution against the tide of prevailing current opinion."

At the same time, the Supreme Court decided another case— *Idaho* v. *Wright* (1990). In that ruling, the Court set limits on allowing doctors or other adults to testify about interviews the adults had had with alleged child-abuse victims. Justice O'Connor wrote this opinion. She said that the interview has to be conducted in a way that makes the child's statements "particularly worthy of belief." That meant the interviewer could not ask leading questions—questions that seem to call for a particular answer. In addition, the interview should be videotaped if possible.

These cases present the problem of balancing the needs of especially sensitive witnesses—such as children—against the rights of the accused. Most very young children have difficulty drawing clear lines between their make-believe world and events that really take place. Adults often question how reliable children's testimony is. Nevertheless, when young children describe sexual practices or reveal injuries that are very different from the experience of most young children, their testimony may begin to appear believable. Under these circumstances, the skill of the interviewer becomes very important. An accused person must be able to confront the interviewer and offer other explanations for what has been described. This is especially necessary when the only evidence against the accused is a child's testimony.

The Right to Subpoena Witnesses

A subpoena is an official order that requires a person to go to court to testify. It is the "compulsory process for obtaining Witnesses in his favor" that the Sixth Amendment calls for. At first, only the prosecutor had the right to subpoena witnesses. In federal cases, the defendant also had that right. In time, many states also gave defendants the right to subpoena favorable witnesses.

In 1967, this right was extended to all state criminal trials in the case of *Washington* v. *Texas* (1967). Jackie Washington was on trial, and he wanted to have a co-defendant testify. That man's testimony, Washington believed, could help clear him. The Court ruled that Washington had a right to have that testimony. The Court's ruling in *Washington* v. *Texas* (1967) incorporated the right to subpoena witnesses.

Many witnesses are ordinary citizens who have seen or heard something that is connected with a crime. For example, some

A lawyer questions a witness. Until a 1967 Supreme Court decision, not all states allowed an accused person to legally force witnesses who might be favorable to his or her side to testify in court.

witnesses have seen bank robbers or murderers in the act of committing a crime. Others have seen people running from crime scenes or heard gunfire. Still others have been told about a crime by the person who committed it. These witnesses are just people who happen to know something about a crime.

There are other kinds of witnesses, known as expert witnesses. Some may be experts in studying fingerprints. Others may know about DNA, the special chemicals in the body that each person inherits. Many scientists believe that each person's DNA is different from everyone else's, but they have just begun to investigate ways to identify DNA. Other specialists may be experts in studying arson (the crime of setting fires). Still others may know about poisons, handwriting, or other specialized areas. Most expert witnesses are paid to testify at trials. Does the state have to pay for expert witnesses to testify at the trials of poor defendants? Is that part of the right of "compulsory process for obtaining Witnesses in his favor"?

Over the years, the Court has had to rule on such questions. Although poor defendants have the right to court-paid counsel, the government doesn't have to pay for investigations or for paid expert witnesses of the kind that wealthy defendants can afford.

Juvenile Justice

Justice for young people presents special problems. Special juvenile courts have been set up to deal with offenses committed by young people. Even in the early 1960s, these courts did not have the usual trial procedures with accusations and confrontation of witnesses. Often there was no counsel.

The idea behind separate juvenile courts is that young people would benefit from a setting that is less formal than that found in the adult trial. Young people are sent to places like reform schools instead of to adult jails. Reform schools were set up to help young people reform, or change, and become good citizens who won't follow a life of crime. But in the separate juvenile system, young people don't enjoy the rights that adults would have in similar circumstances. Also, some reform schools are very much like jails.

Gerald Francis Gault was fifteen years old in 1964 when the sheriff of Gila County, Arizona, took him into custody. His parents were both at work at the time, and they weren't told that he had been arrested. When Gerald didn't show up for dinner, his older brother went to look for him. A neighbor told the brother where Gerald was, and the mother and brother went to the detention home where Gerald was being held.

The young man hadn't been told what the charges against him were. He wasn't told that he had the right to remain silent, and he

Juvenile court proceedings do not follow all the same rules as those of criminal trials of adults.

wasn't told of any right to counsel. He didn't have a chance to confront any witnesses against him.

Gerald was on probation at the time. (Probation is a system that allows people who have been found guilty to remain free as long as they behave well.) Gerald had been in the company of another boy who had stolen a wallet several months earlier.

Gerald didn't know why he had been arrested. It was because a neighbor named Mrs. Cook had complained about him. She said that he had made a "lewd or indecent" telephone call to her. If an adult had made an indecent phone call and been found guilty, the punishment would have been a $5 to $50 fine, or imprisonment for up to two months. Juvenile court judges have much more leeway in deciding what to do. The judge decided that Gerald was a "delinquent child" and sent him to the State Industrial School until he reached the age of twenty-one or was legally discharged. In other words, Gerald would be locked up for up to six years.

Mrs. Cook didn't testify or even appear at Gerald's trial. The judge said that "she didn't have to be present at that hearing." So Gerald didn't have the right to confront the only witness against him. The judge didn't speak to Mrs. Cook either.

When the judge was later asked "under what section of . . . the code you found the boy delinquent?" he couldn't give a clear answer other than that Gerald was "habitually involved in immoral matters."

When the case reached the Supreme Court in 1967 as *In re Gault* ("in the matter of Gault"), the appeal was based on the fact that Gerald Gault had been denied the following basic rights:

1. Notice to the charges;
2. Right to counsel;
3. Right to confrontation and cross-examination;
4. Privilege against self-incrimination;
5. Right to a transcript of the proceedings; and
6. Right to appellate review [review in appeals court]

The Supreme Court agreed that Gerald Gault had been denied these rights. It added that the entire juvenile court system should be reexamined. There were many repeaters (people who were constantly being sent back after being discharged) among the juveniles. For this reason, the claims that young people gain benefits from a separate system were open to question.

The Supreme Court quoted an earlier decision: "Neither man nor child can be allowed to stand condemned by methods which flout constitutional requirements of due process of law."

The Changing Court

"No State shall infringe [violate] the equal rights of conscience, nor the freedom of speech, or of the press, or of the right of trial by jury in criminal cases."

JAMES MADISON

James Madison, the author of the federal Bill of Rights, suggested the sentence quoted above as an amendment to the Constitution. That amendment was eliminated even before the states could vote for or against it. The only part of the sentence that involved Sixth Amendment rights was the right to a jury trial in state criminal cases. But the states didn't want the Constitution to tell them what they could or couldn't do.

Madison would probably be amazed at the way those rights have now been made to apply to the states. Although he had suggested an amendment that would make some rights apply to the states, he didn't include all the federal rights.

Partly because of the lack of any wording that applied to the states, the early Supreme Court heard few cases involving the Bill of Rights, and those were generally federal cases. *Barron* v. *Baltimore*, which the Court decided in 1833, established the principle that state cases were tried by state rules and federal cases were tried by federal rules.

The rights protected by the Sixth Amendment have helped Americans move toward the goal carved above the entrance of the Supreme Court building: "Equal Justice Under Law."

The Supreme Court has changed a great deal since John Jay became its first chief justice and just three associate justices showed up for the opening sessions in February 1790. During the early years of the United States, people were greatly concerned about the possibility that the federal government would become too powerful. The states had created the nation; the nation had not created the states—at least not the original thirteen states. The first Supreme Court justices had lived through the debates about a strong federal government and were aware of the sensitivity of state concerns about federal power.

In time, other concerns developed. John Marshall, the chief justice from 1801 to 1835, was the first person in that position to understand the role that the Supreme Court could play as part of the judicial branch—one of the three equal branches of government. He developed the principle of judicial review for federal law and actions. The Supreme Court could declare acts of Congress unconstitutional. With judicial review, Marshall established for the Supreme Court the place in American government that it still has today.

During the period from 1836 to 1864, when Roger Taney (pronounced TAW-nee) was chief justice, the two main Supreme Court concerns were business and slavery. The Bill of Rights rarely arose in Supreme Court cases, except in those concerning slaves.

Meanwhile, most Americans weren't deprived of their rights. Their state constitutions provided rights. The problem was that a citizen's rights differed from state to state. A citizen who moved from one state to another might find that some former rights no longer existed, while some unaccustomed rights were provided.

Some people expected the Fourteenth Amendment (1868) to "nationalize" the Bill of Rights. But even after the Fourteenth Amendment was ratified, most of the justices didn't believe that it was intended to make the entire Bill of Rights apply to the states. By the late 1880s, the Fourteenth Amendment was being used mainly to help large businesses grow. Few people accepted the notion that it was intended to make all of the federal Bill of Rights apply to the states.

Yet the seed had been planted, and Justice John Marshall Harlan I—on the Court from 1877 to 1911—argued strongly in support of the idea that the Fourteenth Amendment intended to incorporate the federal Bill of Rights and bring the states under its provisions. For many years, he argued alone, but eventually other justices who joined the Court agreed with him.

Years later, Justice Hugo Black, in a famous dissent to *Adamson* v. *California* (1947), discussed the history of the Fourteenth Amendment. He pointed out that Congressman John Bingham, who had drafted the Fourteenth Amendment, originally believed that the Bill of Rights did apply to the states. Then someone showed Bingham the Supreme Court's decision in *Barron* v. *Baltimore* (1833), which said:

Had the framers of these amendments [the Bill of Rights] intended them to be limitations on the powers of the State governments they would have imitated the framers of the original Constitution and expressed that intention.

Bingham wrote that when he read those words, he knew that he had to change his original wording for the Fourteenth Amendment. He changed it to say, "No State shall make or enforce any law which shall abridge the privileges or immunities of citizens of the United States. . . ."

To Justice Hugo Black, it was obvious that Bingham, one of the authors of the Fourteenth Amendment, intended to use the amendment to make the Bill of Rights apply to the states. What is more, Black believed that most people in Congress who voted for that amendment also intended to make the Bill of Rights apply to the states.

Yet other great legal scholars disagree. Many citizens find it very confusing when experts on the Constitution don't agree on what the Constitution really means. One reason for the difference of opinion is that some scholars believe that the courts should not make any changes that could be seen as establishing new laws. This idea of the Court's role is called *judicial restraint*. Other people believe that as times change, the laws should change even though basic principles don't change. This idea is called *judicial activism.*

Because of the differences of opinion in the Supreme Court, it took many years to incorporate most of the provisions of the federal Bill of Rights. The provisions that were incorporated now apply to the states as well. The various parts of the Sixth Amendment were incorporated over a period of about fifty years, and today the Court is still making decisions based on the Sixth Amendment.

Cases That Incorporated the Sixth Amendment		
Counsel in capital cases	1932	*Powell* v. *Alabama*
Public trial	1948	*In re Oliver*
Counsel for people who can't provide their own counsel	1963	*Gideon* v. *Wainwright*
Confronting opposing witnesses	1965	*Pointer* v. *Texas*
Impartial jury	1966	*Parker* v. *Gladden*
Speedy trial	1967	*Klopfer* v. *North Carolina*
Subpoena favorable witnesses	1967	*Washington* v. *Texas*
Trial by jury	1968	*Duncan* v. *Louisiana*
Right to counsel in all cases that could have a jail sentence	1972	*Argersinger* v. *Hamlin*

Despite the tendency to incorporate the Bill of Rights, several justices have given good reasons for allowing differences between federal and state laws and practices, as well as among the laws and practices of the various states. Justice Louis Brandeis noted that it is "one of the happy incidents of the federal system that a single courageous state may, if its citizens choose, serve as a laboratory. . . ."

In fact, states have often served "as a laboratory," trying out new ideas for government. The ideas that succeed are often adopted by other states and by the federal government. These experiments involve less time and expense than there would be if the entire nation had to try out each new idea on a large scale.

The Supreme Court has changed a great deal over the centuries. For most of its history, the justices were white, male, and Protestant. Several justices were Roman Catholic. During the twentieth century, justices were appointed who were Roman Catholic, Jewish, black, or female. These appointments reflected changes that were taking place in the society outside the Court.

Changes in society do affect the opinions of the Court. Some are social changes. Others are changes in technology. At first the nation's courts had to make "horse-and-buggy laws" apply to railroads, telegraphs, telephones, and other inventions of the nineteenth century. Twentieth-century inventions brought even greater changes. Television and radio have changed the way in which the public becomes involved in events. Computers influence the availability of information. Remote-control cameras and videotapes have changed the ways in which we communicate.

Our nation has also developed new concerns about the rights of people whose rights weren't a major concern to the majority of Americans in the past. African Americans, Hispanic Americans, and Asian Americans are now being woven into American society to a greater degree. Juries from which minorities and women are purposely excluded are no longer acceptable. They have demanded that rights be equally applied. Beginning in 1869 in the Wyoming Territory, women had been gaining the right to vote at the local and state levels. In 1920, women, by means of the Nineteenth Amendment, gained the right to vote in national elections. Since that time, women have found a larger role in the world of work and rights. They can no longer be left off juries or judges' benches.

As the twenty-first century approaches, the Supreme Court will have new cases to consider and new aspects of the Bill of Rights to address.

A Speedy and Public Trial

As radio, television, and other media report crimes and keep them in the public's mind, it becomes more and more important for defendants to be brought to trial as soon as possible so that their guilt or innocence can be determined. The Supreme Court may have to deal with cases that are "tried in the media." When juries make decisions that don't reflect the opinions of the media, the public often feels that justice hasn't been served. Somehow the Court will have to maintain a balance between the defendant's rights and claims of the public's "right to know."

Some states have begun to permit television cameras inside courtrooms. Television stations may broadcast or tape an entire trial or just use short newsclips on their news programs. These newsclips, however, don't provide the entire picture of what happens at a trial. The public may get a distorted impression of what took place. The Supreme Court may have to decide cases involving television in the nation's courtrooms.

Impartial Jury

Pretrial publicity often raises the question of whether an impartial jury can be found. In addition, in many states, lawyers have the right to disqualify a certain number of possible jurors without giving a reason. When all the jurors disqualified in this manner belong to a minority group or are women, questions are raised about whether the jury was impartial. The Court has heard such cases and will probably hear others.

State and District

As people move around more and commit crimes through electronic means, there may be an increasing number of courts that must decide where a case should be tried. Many multistate cases become federal cases. When they don't, more than one state may try a defendant for the same crime—part of which was committed in one state, part in another. Sometimes state and federal courts try the same person for different parts of the same crime. The Court has already heard cases about possible double jeopardy, and such cases may continue.

Knowing the Nature of the Accusation

People have a right to know the nature and cause of the accusation against them. This means that an accused person has a right to know what crime he or she is accused of having committed. It also means that an identifiable (clearly spelled-out) crime has to have been committed, and the law has to give clear information about what actions are a crime.

The juvenile justice system has sometimes been at fault in not letting young people know what crimes they have been accused of committing. The case of *In re Gault* (1967) confronted that problem. Immigrants may also be unaware of their right to know the charge if they are arrested.

Confrontation

The 1990 cases involving very young children who were allowed to testify by closed-circuit television raises new issues about confrontation. Will young children's testimonies be allowed to be excluded from the rules of facing one's accuser? Will other people be allowed to testify by television so that they don't have to travel to a courtroom?

Other confrontation issues may involve the testimony of undercover agents who come to the courtroom but are allowed to testify in ways that hide their identity.

The Right to Call Witnesses

The Supreme Court has decided that the state doesn't have to pay the fees of expert witnesses for poor defendants. Yet paid witnesses are allowed to testify for people who can afford them.

The federal government has also established a witness-protection program for witnesses who fear that their lives are in danger because of their testimony. After these witnesses testify, the federal government allows them to change their identity and live somewhere else under federal protection. Some of these protected witnesses later commit crimes. The Court may have to balance the rights of such witnesses against the rights of the public.

Juvenile Rights

The rights of young people aren't mentioned in the Sixth Amendment. But the Supreme Court has already had to decide cases that consider whether young people who have been accused of crimes have the same rights to counsel and to impartial juries and have the same rights to know the accusations and to confront witnesses that adults have. Will more such cases arise?

Sixth Amendment rights began to be incorporated during the 1930s. It is hard to understand why certain rights that weren't recognized before suddenly became recognized. Perhaps the experience of the Great Depression made the justices more sensitive to the needs of the poor. Perhaps the experience of two world wars made people realize that the rights of Americans are what make the United States special.

While some people applaud the acceptance of the "nationalized" Bill of Rights, others are concerned. They feel that the balance of rights has been placed on the side of criminals instead of on the side of law enforcement. These people point to the criminals who have been allowed to go free and end up repeating their criminal actions. Meanwhile, those in favor of the newly recognized rights point to the innocent people who have been convicted. There are good arguments on both sides.

The Supreme Court's decisions strongly reflect the basic values of the justices who serve on it. While each Court has some "conservatives" who argue for judicial restraint and some "liberals" who argue for more judicial activism, each justice tends to be more liberal or conservative on some issues than on others.

When Earl Warren was chief justice, the "Warren Court" gained a reputation for being very liberal. Yet some Sixth Amendment rights were incorporated before Warren joined the Court. The *Powell* v. *Alabama* (1932) decision was made when Charles Evans Hughes, a moderate conservative, was chief justice. Other Sixth Amendment rights were incorporated after the Warren Court, during the time of the supposedly more conservative "Burger Court," when Warren Burger was chief justice.

Many people believe that the "Rehnquist Court," under Chief Justice William Rehnquist, is returning to a conservative position of judicial restraint. Yet it was the Rehnquist Court that made the

The justices of the Supreme Court of the United States soon after David H. Souter (top right) joined it. The "Rehnquist Court," as it is often called after William H. Rehnquist, Chief Justice of the United States since 1986, has ruled in general in a more conservative fashion than the "Warren Court" of 1953 to 1969.

1990 decision allowing children to avoid testifying in the court-room by using closed-circuit television.

Courts are difficult to predict. Nobody really knows what questions involving the Sixth Amendment will arise in the years ahead. All we can do is watch.

IMPORTANT DATES

1215 King John of England signs Magna Carta.

1689 William and Mary sign the English Bill of Rights.

1776 Virginia adopts the Virginia Declaration of Rights.

1791 Federal Bill of Rights is ratified.

1833 *Barron* v. *Baltimore*. The Supreme Court decides that the federal Bill of Rights does not apply to the states.

1868 The Fourteenth Amendment is ratified.

1884 *Hurtado* v. *California*. The Supreme Court decides that the right to counsel doesn't apply to state trials.

1932 *Powell* v. *Alabama*. The Supreme Court decides that the right to counsel applies to states when a capital case is involved.

1935 *Norris* v. *Alabama*. The Supreme Court decides that the right to an impartial jury means that juries cannot exclude African Americans.

1937 *Palko* v. *Connecticut*. Justice Cardozo suggests that there are some "fundamental" rights.

1942 *Betts* v. *Brady*. The Supreme Court decides that the right to counsel is not binding on states in noncapital cases.

1948 *In re Oliver*. The Supreme Court rules that a state may not sentence a defendant without a public trial.

1957 *Mallory* v. *United States*. The Supreme Court rules that states may not have unnecessary delays before an arraignment.

1961 *Hoyt* v. *Florida*. The Supreme Court rules that a state does not have to call women for jury duty.

1963 *Gideon* v. *Wainwright*. The Supreme Court overturns *Betts* v. *Brady* and extends the right of counsel to the states.

1964 *Escobedo* v. *Illinois*. The Supreme Court incorporates the right to the assistance of counsel before a trial.

1965 *Pointer* v. *Texas*. The Supreme Court incorporates the right to confront witnesses.

1966 *Parker* v. *Gladden*. The Supreme Court guarantees the right to an impartial jury.

1966 *Miranda* v. *Arizona*. The Supreme Court guarantees the right to counsel before questioning.

1967 *Klopfer* v. *North Carolina*. The Supreme Court guarantees the right to a speedy trial in state cases.

1967 *Washington* v. *Texas*. The Supreme Court incorporates the right to call favorable witnesses.

1967 *In re Gault*. The Supreme Court says juveniles have the right to due process of the law.

1968 *Duncan* v. *Louisiana*. The Supreme Court declares that a jury trial in criminal cases is basic to due process.

1972 The Supreme Court decides that a jury decision doesn't have to be unanimous if state court juries have more than six members.

1972 *Argersinger* v. *Hamlin*. The Supreme Court incorporates the right to counsel for any trial that could end in a prison sentence.

1975 *Taylor* v. *Louisiana*. The Supreme Court overturns *Hoyt* v. *Florida* by deciding that states are required to call women for jury duty.

1990 The Supreme Court considers cases involving young children as witnesses.

1990 The Supreme Court tries to balance freedom of the press with the right to a fair trial in the *CNN–Noriega* case.

$\mathscr{G}$LOSSARY

amendment   A change in the Constitution.

appeal   To refer a case to a higher court to review the decision of a lower court.

arraignment   A process in which the accused person is brought before a court to plead to the criminal charge against him or her. The accused person is asked to plead guilty or not guilty.

capital crime   A very serious crime in which the accused can be given the death sentence if he or she is found guilty.

co-defendant   A person who is charged with the same crime or complaint as another person.

concurring opinion   A separate opinion delivered by one or more judges that agrees with the majority opinion's decision but offers different reasons for reaching that decision.

contempt of court   The showing of disrespect for a court or acting in such a way as to embarrass, slow down, or stop a court from doing its work.

continuance   The postponement of a trial or other legal proceeding to another time.

counsel   A lawyer who may appear on behalf of a person in civil or criminal trials or other legal proceedings.

criminal anarchy   Calling for the overthrow of organized government by force and violence or other unlawful means.

criminal trespass   The crime of illegally entering or secretly remaining in a building or on another's property.

defendant   The accused, who must defend himself or herself against a formal charge. In criminal cases, this means the person officially accused of a crime.

dissenting opinion   An opinion by one or more of a court's judges that disagrees with a majority opinion.

double jeopardy   The putting of a person on trial for a crime for which he or she has already been put on trial.

executive branch   The branch or part of the government that carries the laws into effect and makes sure they are obeyed.

expert witness   Someone who is called to testify because he or she has education or special knowledge about a particular subject. Such a person helps a jury understand complicated and technical subjects that ordinary people may not otherwise understand.

ex post facto **laws**   Laws that make illegal particular actions that took place before the passage of the law.

federalism   The relationships between the states and the federal government, each having certain special powers and sharing others.

grand jury   A group of from twelve (or sixteen in federal grand juries) to twenty-three citizens whose task is to decide whether there is enough evidence for a trial. It does not decide whether or not a person is guilty.

impartial jury   A jury that does not take sides or form an opinion on a case before the trial begins. The members of such a jury are influenced only by legal evidence produced during the trial. They base their decision on the evidence connecting the defendant with the crime charged.

incorporation   The process of making the rights in the Bill of Rights apply to the states so that people are guaranteed to be safeguarded against state actions that might violate their rights. The Fourteenth Amendment's due process clause is used as the basis for incorporation.

indictment   A grand jury's written accusation naming the person charged with a crime and charging that person with the crime.

information   A written accusation presented not by a grand jury but by a public prosecutor and charging a person with a crime.

interrogate   To question (by police) a person suspected of or arrested for a crime.

judicial activism   The belief or policy that as times change the laws should change, even though basic principles don't. According to this, judges should therefore be free to favor or apply new social policies not always in agreement with previous court decisions. In some cases, opponents of judicial activism claim that such new decisions are involved in lawmaking or executive matters.

judicial branch   The part or branch of the government that interprets the laws and settles disputes under the law.

judicial restraint   The belief or policy that judges should not apply their own personal views or ideas that may not be consistent with existing laws or court decisions when they are deciding a case. The belief is that courts should not make any changes that could be seen as establishing new law.

judicial review   The power of the courts to review the decisions of other parts or levels of the government. Courts may review the decisions of lower courts and come to a different decision.

jurisdiction   The power of a court to decide a legal matter.

legislative branch   The part or branch of the government that makes the laws.

majority opinion   The statement of the opinion of a court in which the majority (more than half of those who vote) of its members join.

mistrial   A trial that has ended before its normal end because something is basically wrong with the pretrial or trial proceedings. A judge may declare a mistrial for a number of reasons. Among such reasons are incorrect choosing of jurors, death of a juror or lawyer, a judicial error that cannot be corrected during the trial, or a jury that cannot agree on a verdict.

plea bargaining   The process in which an accused person and the prosecutor in a criminal case work out an agreement that the court approves of. There is no jury trial. Plea bargaining usually involves the defendant's pleading guilty to a lesser crime or only part of the list of charges in the indictment. In return, the accused gets a lighter sentence.

precedent   A previous decision of a court that is used as an example of or powerful reason for the same or a similar decision in a new case that is similar in facts or legal principles.

probation   A sentence imposed for a crime whereby a convicted criminal is released under the supervision of a probation officer instead of being put in prison. The defendant must behave well—or he or she will go to prison.

public prosecutor   A lawyer who works for the government (such as a state's attorney or district attorney) and tries to prove that the accused person is guilty of the crime charged.

ratification   Approval of an amendment to the Constitution by three-fourths of state legislatures or conventions (after the amendment has been officially proposed by two-thirds of each house of Congress or proposed by a convention called by two-thirds of the states).

self-incrimination   Acts or words before or during a trial in which a suspect or an accused person admits some sort of involvement in a crime. The Fifth Amendment protects people against being *forced* to say they have committed a crime.

separation of powers   The division of the government into three parts, or branches—the legislative, the executive, and the judicial.

sequester   To keep jurors from having any contact with the public during a trial. This prevents jurors from hearing rumors, opinions, or information that is not part of the trial.

subpoena   A legal order for a person to appear in court and testify.

suspect   A person believed to be involved in a crime.

testify   In a legal proceeding such as a trial, to give evidence after taking an oath or affirmation.

venue   The neighborhood, place, district, or county in which an injury or crime took place.

verdict   The official decision of a jury.

witness   A person whose statements under oath are received as evidence for any purpose.

witness protection program   A federal program that secretly moves, changes the identity of, or otherwise protects witnesses or possible witnesses involved in trials or other legal proceedings. This may happen when the case involves organized crime activity or other serious crimes.

$\mathscr{S}$UGGESTED $\mathscr{R}$EADING

*American Political Science Association and American Historical Association, ed. *This Constitution: From Ratification to the Bill of Rights.* Washington, D.C.: Congressional Quarterly, 1988.

The Bill of Rights and Beyond: A Resource Guide. The Commission on the Bicentennial of the United States Constitution, 1990.

*Brant, Irving. *The Bill of Rights: Its Origin and Meaning.* Indianapolis: Bobbs-Merrill, 1965.

Carter, Dan T. *Scottsboro: A Tragedy of the American South*, rev. ed. Baton Rouge: Louisiana State University Press, 1979.

*Cox, Archibald. *The Court and the Constitution.* Boston: Houghton Mifflin, 1987.

*Kohn, Bernice. *The Spirit and the Letter: The Struggle for Rights in America.* New York: Viking Press, 1974.

*Lewis, Anthony. *Gideon's Trumpet.* New York: Vintage Books, 1964.

*Lindop, Edmund. *The Bill of Rights and Landmark Cases.* New York: Franklin Watts, 1989.

*Miers, Earl Schenck. *The Bill of Rights.* New York: Grosset & Dunlap, 1968.

*Petracca, Mark P. "What Every Student Should Know About the Bill of Rights." *The Political Science Teacher* 3 (Spring 1990): pp. 10–12.

Schwartz, Bernard. *The Great Rights of Mankind: A History of the American Bill of Rights.* New York: Oxford University Press, 1977.

*Readers of *The Sixth Amendment* by Eden Force will find these books particularly readable.

$\mathcal{S}$OURCES

Abernathy, M. Glenn. *Civil Liberties Under the Constitution,* 4th ed. Columbia: University of South Carolina Press, 1977.

Abraham, Henry J. *Freedom and the Court: Civil Rights and Liberties in the United States,* 5th ed. New York: Oxford University Press, 1988.

Barth, Alan. *The Rights of Free Men: An Essential Guide to Civil Liberties.* New York: Alfred A. Knopf, 1984.

Brant, Irving. *The Bill of Rights: Its Origin and Meaning.* Indianapolis, Ind.: Bobbs-Merrill Company, 1965.

Carter, Dan T. *Scottsboro: A Tragedy of the American South,* rev. ed. Baton Rouge: Louisiana State University Press, 1979.

Corwin, Edward S. *The Constitution and What It Means Today.* Revised by Harold W. Chase and Craig R. Ducat. 14th ed. Princeton, N.J.: Princeton University Press, 1978.

Cox, Archibald, Mark DeWolfe Howe, and J. R. Wiggins. *Civil Rights, the Constitution, and the Courts.* Cambridge, Mass.: Harvard University Press, 1967.

Crews, Kenneth D. *Corwin's Constitution: Essays and Insights of Edward S. Corwin.* New York: Greenwood Press, 1986.

Cushman, Robert F. *Leading Constitutional Decisions,* 17th ed. Englewood Cliffs, N.J.: Prentice-Hall, 1987.

Dorsen, Norman, ed. *The Rights of Americans: What They Are—What They Should Be.* New York: Pantheon Books, 1971.

Douglas, William O. *A Living Bill of Rights.* New York: Doubleday & Company, 1961.

Edelman, Martin. *Democratic Theories and the Constitution.* Albany, N.Y.: State University of New York Press, 1984.

Fellman, David. *The Defendant's Rights Today.* Madison: University of Wisconsin Press, 1976.

Greenhouse, Linda. "Child Abuse Trials Can Use Television," *New York Times,* June 28, 1990, p. A1.

Hamilton, Alexander, James Madison, and John Jay. *The Federalist or the New Constitution.* New York: Dutton, 1965.

Hand, Learned. *The Bill of Rights: The Oliver Wendell Holmes Lectures 1958.* Cambridge, Mass.: Harvard University Press, 1958.

Heller, Francis H. *The Sixth Amendment to the Constitution of the United States.* New York: Greenwood Press, 1969.

Holder, Angela Roddey. *The Meaning of the Constitution*. New York: Barron's Educational Series, 1987.

Kelly, Alfred H., and Winfred A. Harbison. *The American Constitution: Its Origins and Development,* 5th ed. New York: W.W. Norton & Company, 1976.

Kohn, Bernice. *The Spirit and the Letter: The Struggle for Rights in America*. New York: Viking Press, 1974.

Kolbert, Elizabeth. "Restrictions Put on Right to a Lawyer." *New York Times,* July 3, 1990, p. B1.

Konvitz, Milton R. *Bill of Rights Reader: Leading Constitutional Cases,* 5th ed., rev. Ithaca, N.Y.: Cornell University Press, 1982.

Lewis, Anthony. *Gideon's Trumpet*. New York: Vintage Books, 1964.

Lewis, Neil. "The Noriega Tapes in the Court's Court." *New York Times,* November 25, 1990, Sec. 4, p. 4.

Lindop, Edmund. *The Bill of Rights and Landmark Cases*. New York: Franklin Watts, 1989.

Meyer, Howard N. *The Amendment That Refused to Die*. Radnor, Pa.: Chilton Book Company, 1973.

Miers, Earl Schenck. *The Bill of Rights*. New York: Grosset & Dunlap, 1968.

Nelson, William E. *The Fourteenth Amendment: From Political Principle to Judicial Doctrine*. Cambridge, Mass.: Harvard University Press, 1988.

Padover, Saul K. *The Living U.S. Constitution*, 2nd rev. ed. by Jacob W. Landynski. New York: New American Library, 1983.

Posner, Richard A. *The Federal Courts: Crisis and Reform*. Cambridge, Mass.: Harvard University Press, 1985.

Rutland, Robert Allen. *The Birth of the Bill of Rights, 1776–1791*. Boston: Northeastern University Press, 1983.

Schwartz, Bernard. *The Great Rights of Mankind: A History of the American Bill of Rights*. New York: Oxford University Press, 1977.

$\mathscr{I}$NDEX OF $\mathscr{C}$ASES

$\mathcal{I}$ n d e x

Eden Force is an author and editor of books for young people, as well as of reference books and school books. Among her published works are a biography of Theodore Roosevelt and Silver Burdett Press's *Pioneers in Change* series biography of John Muir, several textbooks, articles for children's encyclopedias, and contributions to dictionaries for both children and adults. Eden Force makes her home in New York.

Warren E. Burger was Chief Justice of the United States from 1969 to 1986. Since 1985 he has served as chairman of the Commission on the Bicentennial of the United States Constitution. He is also chancellor of the College of William and Mary, Williamsburg, Virginia; chancellor emeritus of the Smithsonian Institution; and a life trustee of the National Geographic Society. Prior to his appointment to the Supreme Court, Chief Justice Burger was Assistant Attorney General of the United States (Civil Division) and judge of the United States Court of Appeals, District of Columbia Circuit.

Philip A. Klinkner graduated from Lake Forest College in 1985 and is now finishing his Ph.D. in political science at Yale University. He is currently a Governmental Studies Fellow at the Brookings Institution in Washington, D.C. He is the author of *The First Amendment* and *The Ninth Amendment* in *The American Heritage History of the Bill of Rights*.

Photograph Credits

Cover: Stacy Rick/Uniphoto Picture Agency; 2–3: Independence Hall National Park; 10: © Dean Brown/Omni-Photo Communications; 10 (inset): Colonial Williamsburg; 11 (top): © Brad Markel/ Gamma-Liaison; 11 (bottom): © Dean Brown/Omni-Photo Communication; 12: Michael Stucky/ Comstock; 14: Colonial Williamsburg; 16: "Raising the Liberty Pole" by John McRae/Kennedy Galleries; 18–19: Independence Hall National Park; 28, 31, and 32: The Granger Collection; 41: Collection of the Supreme Court of the United States; 44: The Bettmann Archive; 49: Library of Congress; 52: UPI/Bettmann; 54: UPI/Bettmann Newsphoto; 58: © James Wilson/Woodfin Camp & Associates; 63: Miami *Herald*; 66 (l.), 66 (r.), and 68: UPI/Bettmann; 70: Bettmann; 72: © 1987 Michal Heron/Woodfin Camp & Associates; 75: Ellis Herwig/Stock Boston; 79: S. Allen/Gamma-Liaison; 84: Ira Wyman/Sygma; 87 and 88: UPI/Bettmann; 96: © 1983 Sepp Seitz/Woodfin Camp & Associates; 103: © Carl Bergquist/Gamma-Liaison; 104: © 1985 Lester Sloan/Woodfin Camp & Associates; 111: © Billy E. Barnes/Uniphoto Picture Agency; 113: © 1990 Comstock; 116: © Larry Downing/Woodfin Camp & Associates; 125: Collection of the Supreme Court of the United States.